The Expressive Arts

A Dialogue between Master and Disciple
Avi Goren-Bar Ph.D with Kristjan Černič

Volume II

Dedicated to all my clients, partners, teachers team & students throughout the years who inspired my work.

avigb1@gmail.com

Content

Volume II

Chapter 4 - Jungian Based Arts Therapy
 & Coaching ... 5
Chapter 5 - Object Relations Applied to Expressive
 Arts Therapy & Coaching ... 73
Chapter 6 - Diagnostic Thinking in Expressive Arts
 Therapy & Coaching ... 145
Chapter 7 - Epilogue ... 225

Chapter 4
Jungian Based Arts Therapy & Coaching

Jungian Based Arts Therapy & Coaching

A: Before we arrive at the application of Jungian Psychology to Expressive Arts Therapy & Coaching, I must explain some introductory concepts of Jungian psychology, which are the preliminary basis for your understanding of this challenging font of wisdom, with which I work so intensively in my Expressive Arts practice.

Quite early in my career, when I started to realize that it was essential for me to understand what the artistic object symbolizes, signifies, means, in order to have an archetypal understanding of it, I got acquainted with the immense knowledge of Jungian psychology.

C. G. Jung (1875-1961) was a Swiss psychiatrist and psychoanalyst who founded analytical psychology. His work has been influential not only in psychiatry but also in anthropology, archaeology, literature, philosophy, and religious studies. Jung's psychology attributes to the arts psychotherapy a deep meaning.

For example, there are archetypal movements (expansion, containment, or waves) and those archetypal movements offer psychic content databases. There are archetypal visual symbols. Actually, our dreams are made of them. Understanding the meaning of those archetypes will open up your comprehension of your clients' artistic creations. There are musical archetypes: Heroic, mystical and liturgical, ethnic music, meditative, primal sounds like yelling, humming and groaning. Through the years, I've developed a whole collection of archetypal music to accompany my Expressive Arts practice. The Jungian psychology is my catalogue and dictionary for my clients' artistic repertoires.

K: How does the symbolic manifest in the arts? How are these archetypes connected to Expressive Arts Therapy & Coaching?

A: I will talk to you about Ego-Self and how I apply those archetypes in my Jungian Arts Therapy and Coaching. Erich Neumann (1953), the preferred disciple of Jung, in his book, explains the relationship between the *"Ego"* and the *"Self."* For now, let me just clarify that, in Jungian Psychology, "Ego" refers to all the overt activities in which we engage. "Ego" is our demonstrated conscious behavior. All that we do throughout our daily life: Working, loving, socializing, thinking, acting, operating. If we overdo grandiosely, we will term such behavior as "Ego Inflation." When we speak about a client's "Ego" we do not mean he or she are egocentric, we refer to their daily activities. Now, the "Self" in relation to the "Ego," is like God to Man. The "Self" is psychic-spiritual unconscious potential and wisdom, immense psychic-emotional power, existing in every human being, which paradoxically is located deep in the unconscious (meaning that we are not aware or connected to it in daily life). But, at the same time, the Self encompasses, as a whole, all our existing life. The unconscious, through the archetypes, manifests itself visually. It is necessary here to just tell you briefly that an *archetype* is a visual image which is common to all human beings, and is characterized by strong psychic potential, strong emotional involvement, and composed of two opposing polar traits. The archyetypes function as psychich data-bases and if connected to it properly they can inspire us. The Mother archetype, for example, is associated with birth and nurturing. Yet, at the same time, we bury our dead inside Mother Earth, meaning that it can swallow, capture or castrate us.

When the unconscious reveals its content, it appears in form of wrapped creative ideas, organized or presented in symbolic images that are either visualized in dreams, or manifested in artistic productions. Referring back to an archetypal movement, when a person is dancing, he is dancing through his authentic movement; the Self is expressing itself through the body's kinesthetic images. Archetypal movements can express a big variety of images, such as harvesting, exploding, intruding and rolling movements.

K: I am not sure I understand. What do you mean by "visually?"

A: It means that, when the person moves about, he expresses himself (compassion, rage, freedom, excitement etc.) through symbolic content, and this expression can be interpreted (by him, or by the observer) into a visual symbol. Visual means imagined through a concrete picture.

K: So you or the client can observe a movement and immediately get a concept or image in your head. Is this what you're talking about?

A: Modern ballet is based on this principle. The concept is visual: It's a metaphor, like a picture or a sculpture. When the archetype is expressed on the conscious level, meaning that the client connected through his imagination to a symbol and gave it either a visual or a kinetic or an audio form of expressivity, it turns into a therapeutic essence. These images are the symbols the client innocently produces through making an artistic object. They constitute archetypal images or archetypal symbols. There are internal images for maternity, intrusiveness, connectedness, dependency, freedom. In my Jungian coaching seminars, people connect to relevant archetypes and express them through dancing. They are expressing what they see in their imagination, they are expressing these internal representations, internal feelings and depictions through their dancing movement. The purpose of this experience is to arrive at innovative insights about themselves, just like an analysis of a dream.

K: Why does one individual connect to a certain visual archetype, and another to a different one? What is the difference between them? Is it connected to the individual's life experiences or something else entirely?

A: Imagine that each person has an inner theater. This inner theater features characters, images, pictures, desires may be easily expressed through images. The inner repertoire of every person, according to Jungian psychology is developed from two sources.

Personal Level (Ego, Consciousness, Known)
Archetypal Level (Self, Unconsciousness, Unknown)

The first source is the client's personal story. His childhood, his parents, the culture in which he was brought up, his immediate childhood environment, his life story, the symbols and the cultures that influenced his personal life story. This is the first source. Nevertheless, there is another source, another spring, that comes from a deeper layer of the unconscious, called the Collective Unconscious (Samuels, A. 1986). It is evident that there is a dictionary of archetypes that we inherit when we are born. Unlike the life accumulated personal data (what we actually inquire from our client in the Intake), this unconscious data source is a "psychic DNA." Look at traditional archetypes, such as the symbol of the cross, the wise old man, symbols of negative figures (witch, devil, murderer), of maternity, feminine symbols (the cave, cradle, womb), the tree (a very popular symbol), the sword, symbols of death or life, and many others, all are common to all humans and are imprinted into our psyche from birth.

There is a psychic mechanism which enables us to connect to our internal psychic life and pull out such ideas and images. This mechanism is called the *"Transcendent Function"* (Samuels, 1986). All these feelings, ideas and needs, which are deeply embedded in the unconscious, when exposed through this "psychic elevator" up to the conscious level, for me, they are magical, because they burst out in the form of an image, which is a key to unlock Expressive Arts Coaching or Therapy. This is why we have 40,000-year-old Paleolithic caves of Altamira with pictures that primitive human beings created, presenting the bull as power, the sun as God, and eroticism which symbolizes the "Conjunctio" archetype, meaning the connectedness between two opposites.

K: So the logic is, that if you connect to an archetype, you very likely will be presented with a visual image that brings about emotions, actions, content, ideas which represent either experience from our early childhood, memories or from our collective unconscious. This Image projects out through the archetype in one's artistic expression. Is this correct?

A: Yes. Very good.

K: We spoke a bit about the projection of the internal world outward. What was Jung's understanding of the workings with this internal world?

A: I think Jung would agree that the meaning of our lives is a function of a constant dialogue between the experiences of the Ego (external) and the Self (internal). However, nowadays people are hardly in touch with their instincts, primal needs and authentic expressivities. The media turned us into a global united humanity which behaves, thinks and acts as conditioned by the global media. Erich Neumann (1953) already spoke about the damage that the modern world has done to the human psyche. The more western society developed into nations, into ideologies (communism, liberalism, industrial and later scientific revolutions), the less we value or esteem or connect to human psychic needs. The development of mankind designs the psyche of the individual. A person born after the Hiroshima bomb experiences life differently than a person who lived 500 years ago, or 50,000 years ago, where nature was at its peak power, and people were dependent on the four seasons, in order to harvest and produce life (Harari, Y. 2013). Nevertheless, Jungian psychology, which is called "depth" or "analytic psychology," is interested in the concept Jung coined – Individuation (Samuels, 1986)

K: What is Individuation?

A: Individuation corresponds to the concepts of Winnicot's True Self, or Bollas' Destiny Drive. On these concepts we shall relate in the chapter on Object Relations Arts Therapy. It's the ability of a person to curve, design, and commit to his authentic needs over his personal life. It is a process of self-actualizing an authentic inner repertoire, to become what he needs to be.

Let me give you an example. Tom was referred to me, due to schooling and behavioral problems. At the age of 15, the son of a medical doctor and a school consultant, he dropped out of junior high. Refusing therapy, he agreed to "just come and practice on my drums," as his Mom told me. The ensuing therapy endured 18 months. He established a constant ritual: Arriving, sitting at the drum kit, closing his eyes and practicing. The young man surely had talent. Gradually, I asked him to share with me the visions he had while playing. Later, he agreed to draw them. That music art therapy helped to coax out what he was meant to become: A musician. Once he came to me and spoke of a dream he remembered from the night before, a dream which had stunned him. He reported: "There is a war, and I walk with an army drum across to the enemy. They try to shoot me, but my drumming saves me, as the bullets cannot break through my music." This "Magic Flute" unconscious association gave us the conviction that music is Tom's healing activity. Soon enough, he started a band and, for the next year, he applied to transfer to a musical high school.

People feel miserable, develop psychosomatic symptoms or depression, when they are forbidden to actualize themselves. Jungian psychology deals with the right of a person to become who he needs to be. The psychic database to become who you are is exposed through the connectedness to the Self.

K: So you're saying that the Self is leading the Individuation process through external frustration and internal inspiration?

A: Yes, I can give you another example. Nancy was completely shaped by her family during the former Yugoslav period and its culture, to become an economist. She was the second daughter, and her father had expected a son. She was very much rejected by her family. In therapy, she told me: "School was my rescue, home for me was a disaster." Afterwards, she went to study in Paris, but she didn't graduate, because she didn't get support from her parents. She came back to her homeland, married and gave birth to two children. Thereafter, she divorced, was fine economically, but was miserable personally. She was miserable because she'd never had the chance to become who she had needed to be. In her nature, she is an artist, a philosopher, a liberal person who loves people, creative, but never did she use these assets to connect herself to her authenticity. This coaching now has become a process of Individuation, where she needs to be courageous enough or, in Jungian terms, to move out of her comfort zone and connect herself to the Hero archetype, in order to actualize her life. Individuation is a very exciting coaching process, which needs to be cautiously developed, step by step, because the surroundings will discourage her individualism.

K: If we acknowledge the process of Individuation, and remember the principle of Polarities, which we talked about in the Gestalt discussion, how can we connect both concepts to the therapeutic practice?

A: According to Jung, there are three functions of dreams. One of the three is similar to the principle of Polarities in Gestalt, and that is the *"Compensatory Function."* When we are discussing Jungian psychology, we will use the latter term.

Jung discovered, very early in his writings, that one of the psychic functions is the balancing of the human psyche. When we terribly miss someone, or lack something, we tend to substitute the gap through imaginative gratifications or realistic compensations. Accordingly, when we possess plenty, we might abandon or disrespect it. It's a two-way street. When we are exaggerating with wishing, having, possessing, acquiring, the psyche needs to rest, to let go, to wander and adopt mindfulness – to go into undoing. When we are doing too much, we need to counterbalance this. When we are totally into spiritual and being states, when we surrender to a passive approach, there will be a need, in the psyche, to produce something materialistic. Then the creative archetype will produce ideas. This is amazing, because it gives us a very wide range of life options, as you can go both ways, either to reduce or expand. Rather than discussing this in too much depth, let me provide you with an example.

Emma is around her 40, single, a lawyer and a very hard worker. She is very strict, with high ethical values. She accepted that she will remain a single woman. She gave up on having children, and devoted herself to her career. Nevertheless, she has anxiety attacks that are totally irrational. These anxiety attacks brought her to Expressive Arts Therapy & Coaching. When she started therapy, she unconsciously turned my studio into a shrine, a place to surrender to the irrational aspects of her living. She started reporting her dreams. She was shocked, because in the dreams, she was an active prostitute: She engaged in perverted sex, she walked naked in the streets, "fucked," as she put it, without arbitrary judgment. She was terrified, having no logical explanation as to why she would dream this. In this case, you can see that the compensatory function in the unconscious hit a counterpunch to her actual puritanical real life, which was very narrow, materialistic and not sensational at all. My Jungian understanding indicated to me that this woman connects through her therapeutic process to several unconscious archetypes which, through the compensatory function, flooded her with erotic ideas. Her femininity and sexuality, which correspond to the libido archetype, her trickster archetype, her shadow and the unknown men in her dreams, which represent her Animus (the masculine side of a woman's psyche), were all drafted into the assignment of pushing her out of her rational decision to ignore her womanhood. Possibly the transference towards me, ushering her, observing and participating in her creativity, contributed to the disintegration of her defenses. Emma started to work with clay, which is a very sensual material, and carved out images. She brought life to her dream scenes, which turned into erotic sculptures. I was not surprised at all when she, a couple of months later, reported to me that she had started dating a plumber, who had come to fix her toilet.

K: Why is it healing, to connect to an archetype? Is it so because you're trying to connect to the opposite archetype, in an attempt to balance your psyche?

A: No, it's not as simple as that. First of all, the archetypes and the unconscious operate on the person anyway: In this sense, they are autonomous. You don't need to be in therapy, nor to know Jung, in order for your unconscious to operate on your life. This is how the psyche operates: Life events onset or stimulate the unconscious and, by reciprocity, the unconscious resonates to the Ego level. People encounter, throughout life, all kinds of rituals and crises. A heart attack, an economic breakdown, a disease, relocation, divorce, a child born, heritage, terrible weather conditions, new friendships, all kinds of events can cause breaks in the mechanism of defense and, as a result, the unconscious bursts out. Not only does personal life stimulate the unconscious, but sometimes the unconscious bursts out in its autonomy, because the unconscious is as alive as our physical body. When people come to therapy, to Jungian analysis or Jungian coaching, we are using a natural mechanism that exists already, in order to bring the client into his awareness and understandings.

K: When you say unconscious is bursting out, what do you mean by that?

A: There is a conscious dialogue and a mute dialogue between the conscious level and the unconsciousness. This means that there is an ongoing internal speech, people think inside themselves, people feel inside themselves. Inside themselves there is a chat between your rational doings, copings, thoughts and your desires, wishes, sexual drives, pretensions, fears and anxieties. This entire repertoire is embedded in the unconscious, and appears, to our awareness, as a result of two detectors. One is the external detector, which the subject perceives from the external world. The second is the internal detector that, for certain reasons, because of hormones, biological changes, or cultural changes stimulates the individual.

Let's say someone goes to a cinema, and is subjected to visual external stimuli, which is nevertheless operating on the internal theater of the subject. As a result, the subject can (re)act differently towards the tangible external objects. Maybe because a horror movie was very sadistic, he might find himself making more sadistic gestures towards his partner in life, which will astonish both parties. This is the connection with the Shadow Destructor archetype, which was stimulated while passively observing the movie. Something outside stimulated it, and it became totally autonomous. It is not necessarily something that is under one's control.

K: Is it not under my control, because there is a process of Individuation trying to burst out in me, but I don't always allow it, because of inhibition, my repressive and defensive mechanisms?

A: Yes. However, I think we should connect this with Expressive Arts Therapy & Coaching. The moment you encourage your client to experience Expressive Therapy, you offer the client an artistic stage. Either you ask him to move or to sing or to paint. The moment the client produces art, the unconscious is called to manage the maneuver. It's the unconscious that is the choreographer or the director or the conductor of the expressivity of the human being, meaning that only part of the artwork is what the client has planned, and other aspects of the client's creation axis's productions derive from unconscious interests.

Now please let me refer back to your initial question: Why is it healing to connect to an archetype? The archetype is the authentic knowledge database presented in ourselves in symbolic language. It functions like an inner teacher for life. The archetype comes along as a story in a very dramatic form. Because it is an archetype, it is numinous, it operates very strongly, emotionally speaking. This authentic psychic guide is driving you, pushing you into new experiences in your life, often irrationally! For example, if the client is attracted to a feminine image in a collage he made, and says he does not have any clue why he picked that woman picture from the magazine, it means that he was unconsciously connected, as a man, to a presentation of his Anima archetype (the inner feminine side of a man's personality). Picking or connecting to that chosen feminine figure, personifying her, may eventually allow him to cry, to dare to sing to her, and to be able to express compassion and show patience towards her needs. The client will eventually benefit more from the therapeutic process, because he will develop patience and be able to emotionally process better. The Anima is a feminine psychic guide which leads men to encounter characteristics that may be strange to them. It leads to the development of a new latent repertoire.

In Jungian coaching, I introduce a concept called

"Psychopomp." Psycho pomp, in Greek mythology, is an archetype who takes the dead to the other world. It is the guide of a living person's soul.

It's amazing that, when I ask my students who their Psychopomp is, each one chooses a different leader, according to their needs. One chooses the Hero archetype, another chooses the Shadow archetype, the third chooses the Anima archetype, and so on. Then I ask them to make a contract with the Psychopomp, and we discuss its practical conclusions. Through this revival and encounter with the Psychopomp image, I encourage them to go on with their process of individual inner growth.

K: How do you diagnose the symbolic manifestations of archetypes? From what I understand, they manifest in the artistic expression. But still, how can I be aware of them?

A: This goes according to the Jungian knowledge. There is so much to read about it. There is an endless reservoir of legends, fairytales, mythologies, stories and many books and articles that give us a huge collection of data about the traits of each archetype. The moment you start to develop symbolic thinking, you no longer need to turn back to dictionaries, legends and mythologies, in order to understand how to connect to an Image that represents an archetype. Rather, you start asking yourself, what is characteristic of this Image? Because these images are visual, they have physical traits. If it is strong, sharp, round, curvy, if it represents the spiritual, sky, earth, sea, you ask yourself what it means, and how it is possibly connecting to your client's dilemmas. All the time, you are exploring what this database is presenting to you, considering the assignment to which you are connected. By the way, this approach is relatively new in the West, but in the East, among the Indians and ancient Greeks, people lived their daily lives attributing power and significance to these symbols. These symbols represented the human psychic reservoir (Jung, 1964).

K: Can you provide me with an example? I am not sure I completely understand how you pick it out, diagnose it.

A: In one of our previous chapters, I was telling you about a business woman named Barbara, who was working with clay, and this clay suddenly revealed a swan. I explained this example in detail, how she turned into a swan. If I am asked to diagnose the symbol that came from the clay, the swan, I would do so as follows:

A swan symbolizes a masculine figure, as it has a very long neck. This long neck resembles an erect penis. It is, on the one hand, connecting to water, because it can swim. But, on the other hand, it has wings, so it can fly. It's an archetype that gives us a big range between the blue sky above (the spiritual), and the blue water underneath (profundity). There is a black swan and there is a white swan. When it is a white swan, it shows purity. When it's a black swan, it will hint at a Shadow, at inferiority. The swan usually is the shape of a boat. It can be associated with the Hero quest, moving from one comfort zone to another, unknown side, so it's a symbol for a transformative vehicle. You see, I ask myself, what is this swan, and the more associations I have with it, immediately I say how these symbols, meanings are relevant to the story that my client is presenting in therapy.

K: You have a great deal of knowledge of books, stories, mythologies, and you ask yourself how the symbolic significance from the stories is connected with the client's story. What path does the client's expression lead down? You try to bring up as many associations as you can from your knowledge, and try to make sense out of it, what it means in your client's example. Is this so?

A: Correct, but I want to add here three important comments. First, it is not that important, whether I am accurate. It is important to stimulate the client's dialogue with the symbols that are bursting out from his unconscious. It is important for the client to connect to his artwork from zero distance, so that he dialogues with the image that emerged through the art. Referring back to the Awareness principle in Gestalt therapy, the more the client is aware of his internal language, the more he is connected to his authentic true self.

Second, before I bring my own explorations of symbolism, I ask the client for his own free association, because the client has a lot of wisdom, common sense and life experience. The client is also influenced by the culture in which he grew up. The swan might, therefore, have a different meaning to me than it does to the client. I lean on the client's knowledge.

Third, unlike a hundred years ago, the collective unconscious is embedded in the knowledge of the internet. It's enough to search for "swan symbolic meaning," and you will access symbolism from different cultures. Therefore, such rote knowledge about associations, meaning, and symbolism is easy to acquire.

K: You already spoke about archetypes manifesting in the artistic production. You mentioned some of them, like the Anima, Hero and Shadow. Can you familiarize me with the most prominent ones?

A: One of the most erotic and magical experiences that I go through, while working in Expressive Arts Therapy & Coaching, are those moments when my clients finish the Creation Axis and present their Main Theme. I am always excited and impressed to see how the artistic product encompasses those basic archetypes Jung is talking about. When I look at it, I observe, and sometimes I have to meditate a bit on it, but immediately I see that, under the graphical line, or the artistic assemblage, or in the movement or chosen melody, there are hidden archetypes that are kind of whispering to me: "Hello you discovered me, bring me to the awareness of your client." As a therapist, I need to make this connection, because my client often doesn't see it. Clients produce art with innocence. When they go through the Creation Axis, they are so much involved in the technical production, that they do not heed (even if they already have a predefined idea of the theme) that the archetype is hiding inside the defined theme. This archetype wishes to be discovered.

For example, if a man is making any kind of container, a jar, a big fruit, a big stomach, a fortress, a goddess with huge breasts, an attractive woman, it means that the client is connected to his Anima, or to a feminine entity, which is expressing itself through this artistic symbol.

K: This is exactly what I am interested in. You mentioned that Anima is the feminine inner personality of the male. Can you elaborate a bit more on it?

A: Jung and wife Emma (1974) conceptualized the psychic phenomena of the Anima and Animus archetypes. For Jung, Man's emotional approach to life derives from the Anima archetype. Watch the 2011 Cronenenberg movie *A Dangerous Method*. Upon being excluded from the psychoanalytic society by Freud, Jung discovered an alchemical book called the Rosarium. In its ancient writings, he found a sequence of pictures describing the idea that, in every masculine, there is a hidden, underdeveloped feminine database, which Jung labeled "Anima," meaning, in Latin, "Psyche." Correspondingly, in every Feminine, there is an unconscious masculine database, which Jung called

"Animus," Latin for "Mind." This paradigm, for me, is extremely optimistic, as it attributes to both sexes the entire potential of the opposite.

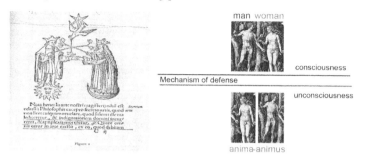

Femininity (in a woman) or the Anima (in a man) is anything that has to do with intuition, nature, vertical thinking inward, introspection, emotion, imagination, compassion and processing.

K: What do you mean by intuition?

A: Jung, in his book *Psychological Types* (1971) described four different types of life experiences, meaning how a person approaches life issues in accordance to his or her preferences: Thinking type, Feeling type, Sensational and Intuitive types. The intuitive leans on non-rational considerations, in times of decision-making and life experiences. These four assets can be developed, but we are born with one dominant type preference, and the others are somehow inferior. When you ask your client, "What did you do in your art," and he answers "I don't know, I just had to do it this way," he relied on his intuition.

K: How can I spot the Feminine traits expressed in an artwork?

A: You will find, in your client's expressivity, the following phenomenological repertoire, to which I attribute my understanding of "Femininity:" The lines in the artwork (this may be also observed in movement or music) are typical of circular roundish circumference.

The client is using nature materials (shells, twigs, dry leaves, dry fruits). The client is expressing compassion, in art this will be caressing, holding together, giving shelter. In movement, it will be expressed by holding the other, containing the other (the "other" can also be objects, such as a ball, a scarf, a pillow). If the art product shows imagination, yet is more intuitive and less organized, not structured nor geometrical, but rather flowing, colorful, with an emphasis on spontaneity and sensational ideas, it denotes connectedness to the feminine principle. It's the same with artworks which are very sensational, using oils or gouache made of thick, heavy strokes and materialistically-oriented. All sorts of weaving, using clay, productions which require longitudinal processes, all those are typical of the feminine (the client is mixing colors and uses colors made as a result of merging or mixing). If the client prepares the material in advance, like the technique of papier Mache (using glue, mixing the glue with water, and soaking pieces of newspaper so they stiffen). In musical production, any meditative or repetitive music will be considered feminine, any ethnic music based on feminine vocal tones.

K: So there are only five traits of Femininity, or are these just the most obvious ones?

A: Your question asks for a dictionary of feminine traits in arts, however let me remind you of my answer to your previous question, when you asked me how I developed symbolic thinking. Here we are, in a derivative of your same question. Instead of expecting a readymade given list, try to find out what is in common with all the characteristics I am specifying for you, under the category of Femininity. Learning to find the common base between traits will teach you to think symbolically. You see, symbolism is a feminine trait, as it requires dwelling in the unknown, the obscure and intuitive. Getting a definite list of traits, a dictionary, a wording catalogue, belongs to the Masculine principle, according to Jungian psychology. When it is totally irrational, like in surrealism, assembling objects together, items which have no logical rules to bind them, it needs to be attributed to the feminine. If a man is instinctual, working with his eyes closed, or with the left hand, or jumping with his legs, creating art which is made through smearing colors on his feet, I will consider him led by his Anima.

Any symbols in art that show transformation: The symbol of a butterfly transformed from a caterpillar, using anything that turns from big to small, or small to big, from inside to outside, any transformative signs are of Femininity. Of course, Anima or femininity will be represented by any symbols of containment. The color red is also the symbol of femininity, because of menstruation, because birth is accompanied by blood, because menopause is losing the menstrual blood.

Symbols of protection are feminine, such as the case of a child in therapy creating a sand tray and putting animals inside cages or caves. Sheltering will also be a symbol of femininity. If a woman displays this repertoire, it means that she works through her femininity.

K: Can a woman also possess masculine characteristics?

A: The idea about masculinity and femininity is embedded in nature and in anthropology. I once heard a Jungian woman analyst, in a documentary movie about Jung, stating that *"we women bare life, you men act upon life."* For me that was it, the fact that we men cannot give birth, nor bequeath a child, makes the whole difference. This paradigm of Animus and Anima is symmetrical to both genders. The Animus is the masculine psychic database of the woman. The Animus can be developed through her relationship with her father, or masculine figures in her intimate surroundings. It can be developed through a traumatic loss of a significant masculine figure, or when she is threatened and must survive. The masculine is typical of speed, intrusiveness, mind, intellect, spirituality, linear thinking, discipline, wording, rationale and physical power.

    A woman who does any kind of art that is three-dimensional, and juts out into space and shows erected objects, a tower, a tall tree, an arrow that penetrates, those symbols denote masculinity. If a man produces some of those symbols, it means he is connected to his masculinity. Masculinity is anything that has to do with precision and time, ideas, order, organization, the rational, altruism, priorities at work, structure, self-discipline, limits and boundaries. Also proficiency, overt meaning, individuality, distinct moral values - those are all characteristics of the Masculine principle. If the client has a need to clarify what he means, wishes to attribute a title to his artwork, present letters or words in his artwork, it hints at the masculine. It has to do with language, with consciousness and insight.

If the client is using, in his artwork, ethical slogans, for example "Be truthful, it will be righteous," it means that he is using a Masculine database. For example, if the client is showing individuality, testifying "my story," "my belief," standing for itself in the art, I will consider this statement a masculine approach. If the work shows a lot of activity, with graphical lines, planned logical lines, it will be attributed to the masculine.

Creating art is a feminine activity based on processing, so encountering "masculine art" is very challenging. If art is very logical, verbal, loaded with meanings, very sophisticated, maybe it's forced art, but it is created from the domain of the masculine principle. If the client compels himself to limits, boundaries, framing, closing, it's considered a "masculine art." If the art is very structured (like Cubism), it is very masculine.

If you see that the client is self-disciplined, puts down contours and doesn't let himself step out from the contours, considers priorities in a specific order, it's masculine.

The art of M. C. Escher is very masculine, because of its sophistication and planning.

Once again, such an artistic style, made by a man, displays his masculine dominance, yet if such a style is made by a woman, it signifies that she is connected to her Animus.

K: You mentioned Femininity (like animals being contained in a cage), and you also spoke about borders and contours, which are signs for masculinity. How can someone like me, who doesn't have experience, differentiate between the two?

A: This is a good question, showing me that you are developing differential diagnostic thinking. If the purpose, the motivation behind the boundaries is nurturing and protecting, meaning they were put in the cage to feed them, or under a tree to shade them from the sun, that's Femininity. But if it's structured so that the animals know where they are, they are classified or designated to separate and not merge them with visitors in the zoo, or the zoo site is geometrically organized, then it shows Masculine consideration. Again, it's all about the purpose and motivation behind the boundaries.

K: How can I use the concepts of Femininity, Anima and Masculinity, Animus in my therapeutic practice? What's the practical purpose of making the gender distinction?

A: Please heed! Not "gender" but "psychological principle," as both genders possess those qualities! I always keep the compensatory function in mind. Femininity/Anima v.s Masculinity/Animus are opposites; therefore, we can expand the client's experience and potential by helping him or her own both traits. If a man's Anima is too elaborate, maybe the Masculinity is underdeveloped. If the woman's Femininity is too developed, maybe we have to compensate for it by developing her masculine side, the Animus?

I usually, in my Jungian teachings, make a graphic presentation of a man on the conscious level, and his Anima on the unconscious level, or vice versa, a woman on conscious level, and her Animus underneath, in the unconscious, to illustrate the existence of the opposing values and qualities in his personality.

This is leading me into something very profound that I want to explain. Our sex is manifested, first and foremost, through our body. In adolescence, when the girl and boy sense the external and internal anatomical changes in their bodies, it is obviously accompanied by relevant archetypal presentations of the anima

– for the boy, and the animus – for the girl. Let us differentiate between the Persona (the social outlook of a human being, the disguise, and the style), and the inner personality, the traits and acts. A person can look very masculine in his appearance, yet may have an undeveloped masculinity (doesn't stick to values, not disciplined). Nevertheless, if you look at his Anima repertoire, sometimes his Anima is developed, but on its negative side. He is hysterical, bashful, outrageous. Look at a woman, who is very sexy, Botoxed and with silicone breasts, and when she walks in the street she turns into a sexual image, yet you may discover that she cannot process, nurture, contain, and this means that she has an underdeveloped Femininity.

When I look at a client, I examine his outlook, but I listen to his story and I try to figure out how the client has developed on those two scales – the scale of Masculinity and Anima, or the scale of Femininity and Animus. When it comes to Clinical Expressive Arts Therapy & Coaching, this structure of the personality will manifest immediately in the way people express themselves.

K: What does it mean, if someone has an underdeveloped Anima or Animus? Why should the therapy be focused on its development?

A: First of all, men whose Anima is not developed, or women with underdeveloped Femininity, find difficulty in complying with Expressive Therapy. That is because their mechanism of defense is rigid, they are reluctant to process, they are afraid to connect with irrational material, and to flow with their intuition.

Men whose Masculine side is very developed (and women whose Animus is very developed), when exposed to the Expressive Arts materials, wish to stay on the rational side and remain permanently conscious. They expect consultation, knowledge, and advice from the therapist. They want to rationalize sequences of events, they want to focus on a problem and solve it. Our challenge, as Expressive Arts therapists or coaches, is to help our clients withdraw into the Feminine principle, for the men to connect to their Anima, and for the women to dwell in their Femininity.

K: I am not convinced as to why one should do this. Let's say I have a very developed Masculinity, and I am happy with it. Why should I also develop my Anima?

A: Life challenges us with such assignments and roles in which the only way to cope with them properly is by connecting to our inferior side, the underdeveloped side in the psyche: A man may desperately need to connect to his feelings, softness, containment, and a woman may inevitably need to connect to logical decisions, use her cognitive learning skills and discipline.

For example, a father tried to impose his severe disciplinary approach on his son, but pushed him to his limits, and this led to his son's suicide attempt. Then, when the child tried to commit suicide, the father refrained from punishing him, and turned helpless and powerless. When the father was referred to me for therapy, he discovered that, unless he was connected to his feelings, emotions, fears and softness – which are aspects of his Anima - he would not turn into a good father. Working in art therapy taught him to process, to be patient, naïve, calm and connected to his imagination. It's the same in business. You can do business from your masculine side, but sometimes you have to connect to your process capacity, or to your nurturing skills, or even initiate irrational solutions, otherwise you will lose the bargain.

K: What happens to someone who remains with an undeveloped side? I think we already spoke a little bit about this, but can we mention examples of pathologies in Femininity and Masculinity in clients?

A: Overdeveloped Animus or Masculinity will reveal the pathology of rationalization, rigidness and, in the extreme pathology, it leads to an obsessive-compulsive disorder. Overdeveloped Femininity, or Anima, will turn into an overly-protective mother, a hysterical man, an over-nurturing parent. It can turn a woman into an intuitive woman, but she cannot study, she cannot master academic studies.

    I shall tell you about Michael, who has been to Expressive Therapy with me for two years now. This young man came to me at age 18, in his last year of high school, and by the second year of therapy, he was drafted into obligatory army service, coming home daily because of mental releases. This client had a very developed Anima, meaning he was very emotional, creative, yet he had a too-developed Anima, meaning he would turn, too often, to hysterical episodes, anxiety attacks and temper tantrums. Other times, he would turn moody and feel depressed. The challenge of being drafted into the army was the main reason he had been referred for therapy. He loved the Expressive

Arts experience, as he was gifted in drama, music and plastic arts. His works were amazing, very expressive and sensational, yet disorganized, associative and too dramatic. After a while, I started to intervene during the Improvisation phase. Always, while he was experimenting with materials, I insisted on him telling me, in advance, what his plans were, to report to me what equipment he needed. What seemed to be a threat to his imagination, spontaneity and freedom, turned into much better art, more intrusive, more declarative, more painful, more masculine. We started to use "tough" materials, such as metal, wires, glue, and then turned to outdoor projects (painting on a wall, breaking bottles and making mosaics out of the shards), where physical power and skills were required. He once said, laughing full of joy: "We moved from kindergarten art into men's art." Parallel to the outdoor art, his negative feminine symptoms disappeared, and his job in the army turned from a nightmare into a bearable duty.

K: So the Femininity or Masculinity can sometimes present the inferior sides of the client's personality, and the need to be developed to create a well-balanced functioning individual. I think you also mentioned the Shadow archetype, connecting to the inferiority of the client? What is the difference between the two? Are they connected?

A: The Shadow archetype has two aspects. First is the negative, evil side of the psyche. This relates to destruction, aggression, addiction, racism, superiority, ruling, wish for power, sexual corruption, all aspects of materialism connected with financial issues, such as stealing, robbing and enslaving.

The other aspect of the Shadow has to do with inferiority. The moment you step out from your comfort zone, from the known, from your skills, from where you feel competent, you inevitably are facing your inferiority. Where you feel weak, incompetent, an underachiever or underprivileged, there lays your Shadow.

The Shadow archetype is comprised then of two negative aspects, one being evil, and the other being impotence. The Shadow archetype can be manifested in Expressive Arts Therapy & Coaching in many occasions: First, whenever the client is facing difficulties, frustrations, feels disabled. Usually, we will face the Shadow in the beginning of the Creation Axis, when the client shifted from one modality to a cross-modality, and may feel uncertain or unskilled. In such moments, the client says: "Look at this, it came out shit," or "I hate such experiences," or "I'd rather not do it," trying to avoid his inferiority. Any criticism of the client towards his own artistic self-product or maneuver is hinting at a Shadow symptom. The Shadow can be manifested through the images that present one's evil side. Monsters, evil creatures, destructive powers or intentions are symbols of the Shadow. The Trickster, the cheater, the liar and the ugly witch. We find Shadow attributions among animals, such as the fox, the wolf, the crow, the frog, the beast, the monster or the dragon.

These evil side symbols all refer to our own negative aspects of our personality. The color black also signifies shadow. Shadow goes with the dark side of our personality, therefore it is projected onto the spectrum of grey and black. Any zone in the artwork painted black, or using black materials, may hint at fear of death, depression, utmost extermination and existential fears. This Shadow issue corresponds to the philosophical dilemma relating to good and bad, evil and purity. Jung dealt with it profoundly, in his book, *Letter to Job* (1952). The Jungian therapeutic approach is to, on the one hand, accept the Shadow side of the personality, to go with it, as it is an inventible, normal part of the personality. Nevertheless, on the other hand, one has to control the Shadow. So we are challenged here with an endless life job to accept the Shadow, but to control it at the same time. Jungians, like Israeli Avi Bauman (2005), would claim that we should go with the Shadow and against it at the same time. Once you conciliate with your Shadow, you put light on it, meaning you are aware of it, and this partial control shrinks the Shadow, and diminishes its manifested acts. Usually, when clients come to therapy or coaching, they wish us to help them reject or have control over their Shadow.

For example, I am working with this adolescent, Abigail. She is acting out through her Shadow, and her parents are terrified. They were shocked that I, paradoxically, did not, unlike them, restrict their

daughter's Shadow. I went along with the shadow. Abigail is trying out lesbianism, and wanted to move to her lesbian friend's house. For the parents, it was like committing suicide, falling into her own Shadow. Paradoxically, I accepted what seemed like a Shadow acting out. Abigail experienced sex with guys, and wanted to try out other sexual experiences. Eventually, we discovered that a severe traumatic loss of an intimate boyfriend had pushed her to the other pole. The moment we "befriend" or accept the Shadow, it reduces its impact on us. In Abigail's case, she tried her girlfriend's hosting option, but returned finally home. In the Expressive Arts sessions, I mostly witnessed Abigail destroying materials, and turning them into a colorful mess, while blasting loud Goth metal music into the air, despite her use of earphones. Often, she would leave the artwork and burst into a violent short dance, collapsing with laughter born of embarrassment.

K: How do you notice evil and impotence in the client's artworks? When do you decide to work with the client's Shadow?

A: The therapist has to differentiate between *"Shadow in the process"* and *"Shadow in the art."* Shadow in the process means that the client is afraid of stepping into the uncomfortable zone. He avoids executing technical skills that he is not accustomed to. For example, she wants to dance a known dance, but not to try to experience a technique which leads to authentic movement, or he is reluctant to even touch the clay, because the clay is "dirty." When the client is very critical or destructive towards himself or his artistic production, we encounter Shadow symptoms. However, it is easy to observe Shadow symbols in the artwork. This happens when the client projects symbols and images which represent personalities or characters belonging to the evil side. A witch, a wizard, a monster,

a hangman, skeleton, torture tools, morbid characters, distorted faces, an altar, a trap, a whip, a belt, guns, ammunition, suffocating, black masks—these are all symbols of the evil side of our personality. This is a sample of the artistic gallery of the Shadow archetype. In the Jungian sand tray, I have specified shelves for such Shadow miniatures.

K: If a client comes forth with an artwork containing such characters, what is the role of the therapist, then? I don't feel that such characters are always bad. They might be evil, but they serve a purpose.

A: The Id, as described by Freud, corresponds partially to Jung's Shadow, in its negative psychic potential. Yet this is underestimating, narrowing and simplifying the high potential of the evil side in our personality.

Sometimes we must act out evil or unethical behaviors, to save or rescue ourselves. In Jungian terms, such acts are done under the term "White Shadow." Indeed, there are times when, inevitably, we have to do something criminal, in order to free ourselves. When we deal with such cases, we must not be judgmental, but rather "go with the Shadow."

In Expressive Arts Therapy & Coaching, and this is very deep in drama and theater, there will be at least one central evil character who is causing the troubles in the plot. In every story, there must be a negative image that has crucial functions in the story, opposing the good guy and, by this, validating the existence of the good. If there is no bad, you cannot define what is good. If there is no Shadow, you have no idea what is light. In Christianity, I guess this role is attributed to the Devil. In the biblical story, it is the exile from the Garden of Eden, due to Eve's and Adam's sins. The moment there is an evil substance, you can start expressing the "Good." Evil's role in the story is to promote the story until the evil is either captured, re-educated, destroyed or befriended by the good force. In therapy, if you want to negate the evil, you are not doing therapy, you are educating. Let me just quote here from Winnicott's statement in his book, *Playing and Reality* (1971): "What is a normal child like? Does he just eat and grow and smile sweetly? No, that is not what he is like. The normal child, if he has confidence in his mother and father, pulls out all the stops. In the course of time, he tries out his power to disrupt, to destroy, to frighten, to wear down, to waste, to wangle, and to appropriate... At the start, he absolutely needs to live in a circle of love and strength (with consequent tolerance), if he is not to be too fearful of his own thoughts, and of his imaginings to make progress in his emotional development." And, later on, he says: "I would rather be the child of a mother who has all the inner conflicts of a human being, than be mothered by someone for whom all is easy and smooth, who knows all the answers, and is a stranger to doubt."

K: From what I understand, when the evil comes out in the artwork, it's not the therapist's job to necessarily address it. The therapist should address the impotent side of the Shadow. With the evil part, he should rather inquire about it, see its function for the individual. How does the therapist differentiate when to see the impotent part and then start therapy?

A: I should rather provide you with the steps I go through when working with the Shadow. First, *acknowledge* that we are having, indeed, a Shadow repertoire in the session. (This is quite a challenge to therapists who, themselves, may prefer avoiding the acknowledgement of Shadow signals).

The Shadow is revealed in therapy, as I have mentioned, either through an image expressed in the artwork, or during the process when the client shows behavior manifesting avoidance of stepping out from his comfort zone, or being critical, fearful, hesitant or aggressive, and refuses to proceed towards facing his or her Shadow.

The second step is to *accept* the appearance of the Shadow. Welcome it. Let the Shadow exist, meaning bring it to the awareness of the client, and mostly encourage the client to express the Shadow through the arts. Either bring to his awareness that his responses display difficulties that hint at the emergence of the Shadow, or explain to him the symbolic meaning of the manifested Shadow image, and encourage him to further elaborate expressively on it.

K: In the second step, helping the client accept the Shadow, how do you know when you have enough trust? What technique do you use, so the client doesn't react defensively or compulsively?

A: I already explained this, when previously we talked about Trust.[1] I use the same techniques as I have explained there.
In the third step, I usually use the Gestalt Here & Now technique, and let the client *become the Shadow*. He becomes his fear, he turns into the inferior symbol in the artwork, or the reluctant feeling which blocks him. He is encouraged to say: "I am David's fear of doing, feeling, becoming..."

In the fourth step, after we succeed, enabling the Shadow to have space in therapy, to actualize itself and explain its role, I *use the compensatory function* principle, and encourage the client's Ego to connect to the Hero archetype, in order to cope with the Shadow. It's a very good method for the client to be a hero in a contained environment, where he can develop his heroic repertoire required for on-setting an individuation process.

To summarize this Shadow challenge, let me share here a recent example about a very dear client of mine, age 56, who confronts beautifully her Shadow, her fears.

---

[1] Read about Trust in Chapter 1

Jungian Based Arts Therapy & Coaching

Her own diagnosis: "The artwork was made during the holidays in the summer vacation, from what I found in the camp. I brought it home and made a dialogue only now.

"The fear is represented by the little eagle-like balls. The stone with the bumblebee represents the path from the bottom that I had to climb, to come to the present state (it leans against the bigger stone, it is not well seen, it is a slope). I made the artwork without the bumblebee, left it on the table and found the beast there the next morning (it was a surprise).

I learned only much later that the bumblebee was put there by my grandson (9-years-old). He thought that it fits there - as simple as that (a real monster comes with going back way, eagles are nothing in comparison to it)

"I am the shell on the feather. The outside represents the outside world. The other shell is in the water.

"The cancer scissors represent the danger, the stones additional efforts to make it to the water."

Dialogue between the Fear & my artwork

Me: You are all around me, like a fence.

Fear: Yes, I protect you. I protected you also in the past, when walking up the slope.

Me: I see that, I feel that – but you also prevent me from moving forward, from moving fast, from moving into the water, which is the natural environment for me.

Fear: My role is to protect you from dangerous, unpleasant things and people, that is what I do – the rest is not my job. If you want my opinion - you are fine also outside the water; you are now in feathers. In the past, you made a few stupid steps when moving, and did not move when needed – your movement compass is not very precise, and far from your well-being. My role is to ensure that you stay good now – when you finally made it to a non-troublesome situation.

Me: There seem to be many of you who create this protective fence. Can you tell more about yourselves?

Fear: Yes, we seem like one fence, but we are many, and each of us contributes his part to strengthen the fence.

Me: Can you introduce each of you, tell me what they think and communicate to me?

F: Yes. Here you go, the top 5.

Fear 1 = Capability Fear: You are at the age where your memory does not work well. It never worked brilliantly, you were never a smart student, just a hardworking one, your average marks were not top scores, you were a neglected child, a late developer, which caused many of your abilities to remain underdeveloped, and now is too late. Once you got very sick because you studied too much, and you cannot afford that, at this age. Your vision is also not good, when you read too long, you get a headache. You need all the free time to keep your body mobile and healthy, otherwise you will turn into a rusty old lady.

Fear 2 = Laziness: You can also call me comfort, you know you never move if you are not forced to do so. In the past, it took you ages to move from unbearable to bearable, you cannot expect that I would let you move from good to the unknown ...there is no real need to stretch me or yourself. Take it easy. ☺

Fear 3 = Opinion Fear: For years, you wanted to change your name and/or your family name, but you did not -you are afraid what your children and your friends will say/how they will comment. I prevented you from making an unnecessary step that will lead you into conflict. At a minimum, other people's opinion makes you rethink your decisions, rethink again and again... So best to avoid this decision-making trauma, and stay in the zone of comfort.

Fear 4 = Money Fear: I am here to defend your current job and its related good salary, as long as possible. You are one of the best-paid people for the risks you take. There is not much risk, you are an appreciated employee who just needs to keep swimming among the rocks of a big corporation. You are a master at that, and I support *you there.*

Fear 5 = Freedom Fear: Deciding on an option will take your freedom away, freedom to do anything, anytime.

Me: Is there a strong bond among the top 5?

Fear: Yes, Fear 1 and Fear 3 are best linked, Fear 2 and Fear 4 faithfully support them, Fear 5 is a bit of an outsider.

Me: If I break the bond between Fear 1 and Fear 3, the fence is not that strong anymore.

K: You mentioned the Ego actualizing itself through the Hero archetype. What exactly is the Hero archetype?

A: This archetype really stands at the center of all human beings' mythologies and stories. This means that it is a current and dominant human life experience. Pearson (1986) describes six prominent styles of heroes we live by. Campbell (1949) has collected all the legends and the knowledge, and wrote quite a lot about the Hero Quest. The moment we are born, we are actually situated on a Hero Quest. By being pushed out from our mother's womb, we reluctantly are sentenced to a life quest. The Hero archetype corresponds with the process of Individuation (Samuels, 1986). Campbell (1949) talks about 17 steps on the Hero Quest, and Netzer (2011) offers as many as 36 of them. These steps, in sequence, characterize different life situations that we all experience, whether we want to or not. The basic steps are the "call for the quest," "refusal" to set out on the journey, "meeting with supernatural aid," "crossing the threshold," "falling into the belly of the whale," "the road of trials," "falling in love with the Goddess," and so on.

K: Where can I notice the Hero archetype in the

artwork? How can I start a significant process with the Hero archetype?

A: The Hero archetype correlates to what I explained previously, about the Psychopomp. Very often in Expressive Arts Therapy & Coaching experiences (either in psychodrama or drama or in the plastic arts, and even in certain movement expressions) the client may reveal a Main Theme which deals with an inevitable Hero Quest. This image in art usually takes the form of a legendary hero, or wise woman, or a royal animal, a graphic holy sign – all of which urge the client to cope with a great challenge. In movement, it may be a new body expression, a directing body gesture, an image occurring as an insight aroused while moving. All those options bring the client to an inevitable understanding that he needs to cope or change something crucial in life. In music, it may be a hymn, a song invented with words presenting a vow. That associated image connected to the Hero Quest must have the qualities, properties and potential to become the client's internal leader or coach. That image, made by the client, is either admired, or possesses a certain quality that the client needs, in order to cope with a faced challenge. This precious "somebody" may be a character symbolizing either wisdom, physical power, materialistic assets or beauty, etc.

    By connecting with this expressed internal leader, the client inevitably turns into a hero himself, as the awareness of the internal leader pushes him out of his security zone, in order to individuate. If we help the client dialogue with this figurine or this image or symbol, and befriend it (crucial to stress that this image was made or selected by the client himself), the client will turn into a Hero, by trying to actualize the expected challenges in his life. Therapy or coaching must reassure and take responsibility to accompany the client throughout the Hero Quest process, so that, on the one hand, he doesn't procrastinate, delaying the actualization of the desired end, yet on the other hand, that he will not risk too much, with over-motivation to achieve the goal. Committing to one's individuation quest may be quite risky.

K: This means that, in the course of coaching or therapy, you see some quality in the artistic production that the client produced, and that artistic quality, if developed, refers to a Hero Quest?

A: Before starting this book, we had several discussions about what I called Masculine Expressive Arts Therapy & Coaching. "Hero Quest" is a defined structure of psychological conditions, typically based on the principle that the Ego must overcome challenges. I think that, when a client faces an obstacle, therapy and coaching must turn him inwards, he must intrude or penetrate his true self by experiencing the impossible, and by this I mean "Masculine," in the Jungian sense. In most legends, the Hero falls inevitably, or encapsulates, or is imprisoned, or descends into the abyss, the Depth – meaning that he psychologically confronts his own personality limits. The purpose of deciphering the Secret in the client's artistic production is given mainly in order to design, for the client, a Hero Quest developmental program. If you speak about change and challenge in psychotherapy, you immediately progress into the Hero Quest territory.

    This is my approach, I believe there is always a hidden Hero sign in the expressive therapeutic process, which strives to be actualized and offers an innovative repertoire for the client's life.

K: Is there anything else you would like me to know about the Hero?

A: The Hero archetype is interfacing other psychic archetypes, and this means that the client, while exposed to one archetype, will inevitably have to deal with other archetypal experiences, as well. When a woman's life pushes her into becoming a Heroine, she needs to develop her Animus. When a man reluctantly is involved in a Hero assignment, he eventually discovers his Anima or Trickster archetypes. Both will inevitably fall into their Shadow, as they face their inferiorities. While overcoming obstacles, their appearance may change, and this will affect their Persona (how they talk, how they dress, what accessories they use). The Persona of the Hero includes a sword, which symbolizes the potential to analyze. The strength of consciousness lies in the ability to sort our preferences, to analyze conditions and be able to decide what is in your benefit and draw conclusions. This analytic process is symbolized by a cutting sword. The Hero's shield represents the potential of containment and warding off, to see yourself reflected in the shield, to be mirrored and discover your inferiorities. Eventually, along the Hero Quest, you will discover your Self. The appearance of a Father archetype figure along the quest presents yourself in face of discipline and authority. By experiencing the Hero Quest in therapy or coaching, we inevitably have to discover and connect to all its neighboring archetypes.

K: Are there any other archetypes you want to share with me?

A: I think it is important to relate again to the "Self" archetype, according to Jungian psychology. The "Self" archetype is quite challenging to comprehand. As explained by Jung (Samuels, 1986, see "Self") and by Neumann (1953), who followed him. Jung related to the "Self" as a very complex and paradoxical psychic structure. At the same time, it is both an internal God image, an inner extreme power in the personality, which has all the intuitive knowledge and the spiritual values in the human being. It embraces the Ego and corresponds to the Ego with what Neumann termed Ego-Self Axis, meaning in reciprocity: The Self transmits ideas to the Ego but, at the same time, is effected by the Ego's actual activities. Jung conceptualized the "Ego" as the human being's whole functioning. All of which covers the different domains of our everyday observed activities, what is reported by others or by us. The Self is the deepest archetype, located at the bottom of the personality. We speak of a person who is Self-centered, listening to his Self, to his inner voices, to his intuition, if the person is in touch with his unconsciousness interprates his dreams, allows himself to be creative, to think irrationally sometimes, does not necessarily conform but rather obliged to his Self. Jung emphasizes that the Self is not only something located at the bottom of one's personality, but rather the Self encompasses, wraps and covers the human being's experience, which means including the Ego.

There are several "Self" symbols which we can see in Expressive Arts Therapy & Coaching. First is light, because it brings knowledge and clarity to the Ego. The light which intrudes into the "ignorant darkness." Accompanying the light is the Sun. Beside illuminating and adding transparency, the sun guards our life through photosynthesis, and because the sun rays are so very fast, the sun is attributed to the Masculine principle: Rapid, linear and dwells in the spiritual sky. The "Self" is also a symbol for development, because the more we grow and advance, the bigger our "Self" becomes. In "Self" symbolism, we shall find the egg, the baby, the baby Buddha sitting on lotus leaves, the Christ child in a cradle, the innocent, they all symbolize potential which, in future, will become heroes, geniuses, leaders, prophets etc. Another symbol of the "Self," which correlates with potential, is Gold, which is considered, in alchemical texts, as the utmost metal among all the metals, and the treasure which is condensed potential. In addition, every vehicle of transportation which propels the hero on his quest, such as a boat, horse, engine, or airplane, are all symbols of "Self" transformation.

Of high importance for "Self" symbolism stands the Mandala, which Jung found to be a deep "Self" meditative spiritual artistic activity. He displays and writes of its importance in his *Red Book* (2009).

The Mandala organizes the Ego around a balanced structure. Anatomically, we are built as a unit with a symmetrical body structure. Our head begins a vertical sequence that terminates with our soles. We are balanced also through twin symmetrical organs. This brings me to believe that every artistic organized expression hints towards a balanced experience. Obviously, the deliberate breakdown of the balance may be an artistic statement. Apparently, one of the characteristics of the "Self" is an absolute symmetry, balance and centering locus. It denotes perfection. When the opposites in our personality are integrated into one unity, we arrive at a balanced tranquil life experience.

In my studio, If I see, in art therapy, any balanced graphical structure, it doesn't necessarily have to be squares and circles, but any balancing, centering format around an inner core, organized around a nucleus, I interpret it as good sign that the client is either connected to his "Self," or wishes to arrive at such a balance. The therapist's job is to bring to the client's awareness his psychic state of mind, and discuss it over the course of the therapy. We may inquire as to how centering, balance or symmetry are essential to the client's functioning in everyday life.

One more vital example for Ego-Self artistic productions in therapy or coaching can be found in Ego-Self art works.[2]

Art which is inspired by the Ego level is *concrete* and conscious: It is comprehensible, obvious, anybody can figure out what the artist meant to express. Usually the contents of concrete arts are overt experiences which the artist observed in real life, the rules of physics and common sense are dominant.

Unlike Ego art, the arts which derive from the "Self" level are *abstract*.

They are open to interpretation or require

---

2 You may read about it in my article on the helicopter disaster in my upcoming book *Expressive Arts Therapy*, coming in summer 2018 Cambridge Scholars Press.

explanation. Surrealism is one example of combined style where realistic objects are deliberatly distorted by self inspirations. They are ruled by imagination and transmit a metaphor very likely not realistic. Such arts cause us to associate, project and merge into the artistic production, bringing our own subjective comprehension to them.

K: You presented brief examples of archetypal symbols that can manifest in the client's artistic production, and can yield diagnostic knowledge. This knowledge can serve as a point of orientation in the therapeutic process. However, I'm still not sure about the leading principle of the therapy or coaching. What should the main focus be when I'm following the Jungian approach?

A: You pose a crucial question. Getting acquainted with the Jungian approach to dream analysis will add further understanding to the practice in arts therapies productions. Dreams and artworks are based on the same mental processes, as they both produce visual images. As I've mentioned, there are three functions for the dream. My experience shows that those three functions can present themselves equivalently in an artwork of expressivity and, therefore, can be used in the therapeutic or coaching practice.

The *first function*, about which we have already spoken, is the *Compensatory Function*. The psyche has a role in balancing itself by providing you with what you don't have, or taking away from you what you have too much of.

The *second function* of the dream is the *Educating Function*. The psyche knows what is good for you, it is always teaching you what should or shouldn't be done. I am looking at this educating dream principle in the artworks of the clients, which means asking what the artwork wants to instruct or to teach my client. Example: In a seminar on sand tray therapy, one of the women, a widow in her fifties who suffered from mild depression (which she attributed to the loss of her husband, 10 years prior), made an impressive tray when, in the center, she arranged a river, on both sides were forests and wild animals. In the river, she located a miniature of Pocahontas in a boat, "rowing against the stream," she claimed. I was astonished that, at her age, she identified with that instinctual nature figurine, who leads her little boat, with one tough paddle, against the stream, against conformity. When asked to dialogue with that heroine, the woman consulted with Pocahontas about new relationships she has started with a young man. We found out that the woman's psyche (projected onto Pocahontas) urges her to go on with that relationship with the man much younger, and move out of her old apartment that she'd shared with her late husband. What a deeply educating message, from such a simple seeming cartoon movie figurine.

The *third function* of the dream is rare, but exists, and it can be very overwhelming. This is the *Predicting Dream*. Such dreams are almost impossible to comprehend, and usually they point to a strong intuition, to events or situations unexpected, and in the far future.

In Expressive Arts Therapy & Coaching, I am looking at the art production as if it is a dream. Both art and dreams appear through the transcendental functions from the unconscious, and both carry visual images. Whatever I learned about dream analysis is based on my Jungian studies, but mostly I lean on Gregg Furth (1988), Hopcke (1990) and Marie von Franz's books (1988).

Now, how those three functions manifest in practice. First, the Compensatory function calls for balance. I am looking at the artwork and discussing the issues with the client. Either something which exists needs to be reduced, or should be added to. If the client is expressing vigorously, with intention, certain content, or if it is too colorful, or some structures or contours are missing, or it's all a mess, then we need to comprehend how this appeared in the work, and later, by compensatory function, we may need to reshape the artwork. Exaggerations may denote that the emotional side is too involved, and the cognitive side is not sufficiently present in the art. Or, for example, if there is a sand tray that is totally hostile (soldiers are killing soldiers, there is no sign of hope or peace), I understand that there is a split where the benign is rejected (no collaboration, no equality, no symmetry in the client's internal life), and then again we need to discuss the significance of the dominant pole, which is expressed and very developed, versus the other pole, which is ignored or neglected.

Please note, if a client is engaged in aggressive acts, it doesn't necessarily mean that the client is aggressive. Another option is that the client is projecting his own aggression or, according to compensatory function, maybe he is a very weak person, a victim, and this is an artistic expression of wishful thinking. This compensatory function helps me understand the need of the client, and also what is missing and what still needs to be developed.

K: When you have an artwork in which there is too much color and not enough lines, black and white contour, how do you know, how do you check with the client that this is not only a momentary manifestation that has nothing to do with the opposite pole? How do you know it's not just a random occurrence?

A: Everything that we experience in the Here & Now session in Expressive Arts Therapy & Coaching is a sample of the mind presenting itself in the immediate, current moment. Our job as therapists or Coaching is to expand the client's awareness, for him to see how it is applicable in his daily life. It doesn't mean that what we see we can immediately generalize and judge with certainty. One's personality has many selves, the personality is a kaleidoscope, and it's changing according to our inner needs and external conditions. When a client is presenting a negative state of mind, we have to check with the Me-Thou technique, in the Here & Now, to see what purpose it serves.

     Assuming a person is now connected to a very sadistic need, this means that, Here & Now, he has to dialogue about it to see what its role is, and how it manifests in his life. Dance the sadist, play the sadist's song, create a sadistic image: These are options to bring the momentary sadistic mood into the session.

K: When you said you pose questions to yourself about the artwork you observe, is this a point where you ask yourself "Is this artwork pointing out signs of compensation need?" Can you ask the client what this is, and if the client responds with a certain answer that corresponds to your initial diagnostic assumption, may you conclude that it's too much in one polarity? Is my understanding correct?

A: Let's look at a client whose artworks are typically and consistently comprised of esoteric symbols, all kinds of mandalas, abstract work that reveals nothing about her daily life, conflicts and desires. We can understand that she is using the compensatory function of one Pole, of abstract language of the "Self," which protects her from coping and bringing into the Expressive Arts Therapy & Coaching her daily problems, which are not expressed in "Ego" art. It doesn't include human characters, cultural and personal issues. This is certainly an option, that by dwelling close to esoteric symbols and spiritual life, she feels safe and fulfilled. If it is not balanced through active and efficient day life activities, I would consider this abstract style a mechanism of defense, meaning that the lady has good enough reasons not to express her "ego dilemmas" in therapy, as she might be terribly wounded. The challenge here is to really find a way, under basic trust, to slowly expose the personal story on an "Ego level" in arts therapy.

K: From your recent example about the "abstract lady," I recognize that her artworks show symptoms calling for a Hero Quest, where she reluctantly will need to connect to the other pole, to the "Ego pole." The client's artistic productions always include manifesting archetypes. Nevertheless, when we talk about the three functions of the dream, that also manifest themselves in arts, they present a wider concept, a leading principle that includes such archetypes. Is my assumption correct, if I say that the archetypes in the artwork comprise a portrayal of the three functions of the dream?

A: Bravo! They are the characters, the actors of the inner theater. The inner theater is telling the therapist through which function the client expressed himself.

K: Whenever the artwork is presented, or during the process, if I sense an inner need that is pointing excessively to one polarity, I can see that it has a compensatory potential. Can I try to bring it to the client's awareness, and if I'm right, can we work on it?

A: Yes! You still have to differentiate between two sources of the client's motivation: A need out of *self-protection*, and a need out of *lacking something in life*. A client who expresses himself in a style characterized by manic defense (using lots of colors, or moving and running about very kinesthetically, or using the musical instruments to make chaotic music, displays one pole of expressivity). It produces an impression that, from one session to another, the client is surrounding himself with one pole of expressivity that is opposed to another pole of being weak, observant, logical and structured. The other source of motivation is a compensatory need to make up, in therapy or coaching, for what is missing in the client's life. For example, a coaching framework might be a place, where one can compensate for a neglected pole. Such is the case of a woman who was referred to coaching, and uses lots of art materials while, at her office job, she is very logical, considerate and economically-oriented.

K: What's the difference in intervention in such cases?

I would guess that, with the second need, the one out of deprivation, there is no need for intervention, and in the first example, there is a need.

A: Correct. The intervention is a function of your diagnosis. If it's a need, let the client have an enabling, supporting environment to fulfill her needs, to dwell in the "celebrating" pole. However, when you sense or diagnose that this chaotic hyper style is defensive, after the client fulfilled so many creative acts on the same pole, the recommended intervention would be to go into the Improvisation phase, and shift the client into the other, opposing polarity. Shift him to improvise on the other polarity, so that the new material he is exposed to will "work on him" to create an innovative creation axis, in a calmed-down style. This is where the Creation Axis is so helpful. If the therapist learns the Creation Axis profoundly, he will notice that, once the client is moving into his inferior function for a compensatory experience, it is advisable to lead the client into an Improvisation phase, with tenderness and patience. It's a matter of trial and error. In the Improvisation phase, after arriving from the hyperactive, intense artistic experience, the client will discover new prototypes, and may show some hesitance, therefore the therapist has to act with the client, so that he becomes acquainted with the new psychic material, in order to gradually advance and arrive at the Main Theme, expressing the other, inferior pole.

K: The function of the Compensatory principle is much clearer to me now, thank you. You mentioned that the second function of the dream is the Educating function.

How is it displayed in Expressive Arts Therapy & Coaching?

A: The client has two teachers or Coach, two mentors. The first is the therapist. This is why they apply and pay for coaching and therapy, since they lean on the expert's knowledge, time and experience. Yet the other mentor is more important. This is the clients' wounded healer, an archetype Jung presented, based on Greek mythology about Chiron, the centaur (Sedgwick, D. 1994).

K: What is the Wounded Healer archetype?

A: Whan (1987) in his article "Chiron's Wound, Some Reflections on the Wounded Healer" tells us that the Greek mythology challenges us with a story where Hercules, while learning to shoot venomous arrows, mistakenly harms his mentor, the centaur Chiron, who is then bleeding to death. Hercules, in a panic, wished to save his mentor, and the wise Minotaur, who was a healer, begged him to let him recover by himself, through his suffering. Jung points out that the healer dwells within us. This means that, inside the personality, inside the psyche of the client, there is a wise mentor of which the client is not aware. This is a presentation of the client's

Self, which knows how to lead the client toward what is best for him. The "Self" knows what is good for the client. Since the client is usually committed to the False Self, he does not listen to the True Self, the one which knows where and how to lead him. Our coaching role is to direct the client inwards, and help his connection to his own wounded healer.

K: Why don't people listen inward to themselves?

A: Usually, what the "Self" is inquiring of the "Ego" is beyond the Ego's comprehension. This is why it pushes the "Ego" into an uncomfortable zone. When I look at the artworks, observe a movement session or observe a client engaged in an authentic musical production, I ask myself what this piece of art is trying to tell the client, what kind of knowledge it is trying to transmit to him. By the technique of I-Thou, dialoguing with the artwork or its components, the client can be exposed to his own internal wisdom, which is expressed throughout the artwork. When the client connects to his inner teacher, because the art is revealing the wisdom of taught knowledge, the client can easily commit to himself, as the knowledge is coming from him. This is so crucial: The arts we express can grant us our own remedy, which is a very useful approach in life.

K: From what you've just explained to me, I understand that all of the three functions of the dream can be present in the same Here & Now therapy. It's not either one or the other, but maybe rather that one is dominant and, at other times, another becomes dominant.

A: Of course. Remember that, for the sake of learning, we are analyzing knowledge, categorizing it in domains, chapters, paragraphs, but the psyche operates differently, it processes on multiple layers at the same time.

K: But sometimes the operations are not simultaneous. Sometime one excludes the other. Referring back to the Compensatory function, we may see only one pole manifesting, and the other one absent.

A: Nevertheless, the inferior side exists as latent potential. It's like undeveloped muscles which need training to grow.

K: If the Educating function is the dominant manifestation in the arts, how can I notice it? Can you give me an example, so I can envision it?

A: It can be a figurine or an image that the client doesn't attribute any meaning to, yet I see there is a profound message. "I don't know why I did this," says the client, and I am impressed as to how the unconscious is leading the client to an encounter with a new message or content or experience. The client doesn't know that a teacher has just appeared, manifested in his artwork. I usually refuse to ignore this artistic artifact, and I give a place to the new image in the session. There are many ways to artistically express an educating message which appears during an Expressive Arts Therapy & Coaching session. Based on the image, we can create a psychodrama by inviting members of the group arts therapy to take over the image and personify it. We can encourage the client to hold an Me-Thou dialogue with the unfamiliar image. We can elaborate on the artistic product which presents the innovative message and produces more versions of it. I can express myself as a therapist by relating directly to the innovative image. Everything is effective, as long as we return to the client and check on how this artistic experience connects to his life, what it wishes to transmit to him, or how this artistic teacher can help him in his daily dilemmas.

If you wish, this internal Wounded Healer issue corresponds to the first two steps in the Hero Quest. When the Hero moves away from his comfort zone, one of the first stations he encounters is "Meeting with a Supernatural Aid." Thereafter, when he gained the target of his quest he often falls into his Shadow (becomes corrupted). Eventually he attunes to the "Father Image." These two stations are connecting to external or internal teachers. By interacting with them, the client is expected to benefit from his personal growth. Often an artwork, a movement session, an intensive musical improvisation, yields strong insights applicable to life.

K: When we are discussing the Educating function of the dream, it reminds me of the 6th stage of the Creation Axis, the Preservation phase, where you ask the client the significant question, "How does this experience connect to your daily life?" Can this be an intervention of an Educating function making its presence felt?

A: This question is one which is totally legitimate, while analyzing the Educating function of the Expressive Arts Therapy & Coaching. If we do not make this question present, the Educating function will not take place, and it will be just another dramatic episode that will not be generalized and applicable to life.

Sometimes I use the group Expressive Arts Therapy & Coaching as a laboratory, where people can really experience new behaviors and ideas in a capsule of containment and support. Based on the assumption that the group is mature and well-established, with strong compassion skills, I may use the group context as a simulation for a Hero Quest, and to encourage the client to experience what the art product expects her or him to become. For example, let's call the scene I shall describe to you as "the sword experience." I may encourage a woman (in an art group therapy) who created an art piece (a shining, beautiful sword) to empower her assertiveness. Previously, in the group, she complained of her non-definitive and undetermined status in the group. Based on the "sword" she made (a phallic symbol), I could ask her to hold the weapon, point that sword at members she cared about, and practice confronting them by telling each of them what she really needed from them. This surely opens up a significant group dynamic of fight and flight, on twin-ship coalitions, on schizo-paranoid approaches, anger, jealousy and other tough issues that are vital, yet challenging to deal with in the group.

K: How about the Predicting function of the dream? How

is it presented in Expressive Arts Therapy & Coaching?

A: It's very rare that people have such a strong intuition that they can predict events or life experiences they never experienced before, and will eventually experience in the future. I don't see many examples and episodes in my Expressive Arts Therapy & Coaching practice. The Compensatory and the Educating functions are those the therapist or coach work on most intensively, the coach leans on them, and they create the hidden contract with the client. Predicting dreams hint at a domain for which the psychotherapy or coaching are not oriented. We are dealing with the Here & Now, and the potential that will manifest itself in the future.

K: We spoke about the symbolic manifestation of archetypes, and the three functions of the dream, which can also show up in an artistic production. This promotes the diagnostic thought in the therapist, which initiates potential for a significant therapeutic session. There are so many things I need to focus on at the same time. How do you structure this diagnostic thought? What is the best principle to gather such information? How do you know when to react to it, or to leave it as a hypothesis?

A: Now, from an integration point of view, you are referring to the therapist or coaching who attends the session as a participant observer in the studio. When I am exposed to a gallery of archetypes and symbols, presented in my client's expressivity, one of the diagnostic roles that I have to hold for the client, one of my crucial responsibilities, is to try and integrate the symbols into a holistic concept. At that moment, the Expressive Arts therapist or coach turns into a copy writer, a theatrical director, a musician, a choreographer, a philosopher, a teacher an interpreter. To my understanding, when I mentioned the Hero archetype that touches on all other archetypes, the same goes for the therapist who embraces, for the client, his inner theater. The integration gives the client a psychological framework with which he can cope with the problem unfolding. This integrative approach, meaning the summing up of all the psychic unconscious data which emerges in the client's symbolism, I learned from Gregg Furth (1988), in his Jungian didactic book, *The Secret World of Drawings, Healing Through Art*.

K: Do you follow the Creation Axis and, if the client presents first a certain figure and then a different one, do you always start acknowledging the first figure, or is it sometimes somewhat unimportant? What kind of process do you follow, when you're creating this story, integrating it in your mind?

A: There are two factors, two compasses that lead me. One is the *chronology* of the artistic production, and the other is the *interaction between the archetypal or symbolic figures*. The chronology means which symbols appeared first in the sequence of the client's expressive experience. Which figurine was put first into this sand tray? What is the first image that came up in the Creation Axis in the drawing? What is the first dominant movement in my client's dance? What is the first song that came up in the client's memory, and what came next, and how do all the parts interact with the first artistic factor? What is the accord of symbols or images that is accumulating?

K: Can you give me an example?

A: Let's say the client first presents a father figure, then he adds a grandfather figurine, and then he puts in a stallion, masculine horse, so all the masculine symbols come first, and the horse is summing up this masculine collection. Then the client lays down a white virgin figurine. This means that his masculinity is dominant, and needs to be presented first, in order to accept and allow the presence of a fragile feminine figure, the young innocent Anima. My assumption would be that only when there is a whole battalion of masculine presentations can the client accept his feminine side.

K: What about the interaction principle between them? How does it work?

A: When I am looking at an artwork, I am looking at the interaction between the components. Do they collaborate, are they opposing each other, do they stand in sequence, are they in symmetry? These criteria tell me the psychodynamic streams of my client's personality. How do they interact? Do they cooperate? Are they antagonistic?

K: I think I will envision it better if you provide me an example.

A: Surprisingly, I shall take you back to my client, John the architect, who is still in therapy with me. He did a sand tray the other day. It took him quite a while to start the sand tray activity. My impression was that he prefers to observe the miniatures from distance, and this gave me the association with what he had told me recently, that one of his few pleasures in life is to sit for a morning coffee in a café and observe people. Thereafter, he piled up a small hill from the sand and put on top, to my surprise, three tiger figurines. Then came a "delegation" of four elephants at the bottom, on the left side of the tray. First extreme aggression on the summit, and then elephants, a huge animal, vegetarian, the symbol of containment, of carrying, of nursing, yet when in danger, they can possibly be very dangerous. Then he added small farm animals, like rabbits and ducks. I noticed there were no human figures, up to that moment. This means that he was in touch and attracted to primal instinct. At last he added a "Tin Man" and a pirate. Did the animals interact? No, he simply demonstrated power and cruelty. What is the meaning of a figure that presents a lack of emotions, like the Tin Man and a pirate, who lacks family, homeland and lives on robbery? John was exposing, in this sand tray, a presentation of his latent Shadow. By integrating the symbolic repertoire of all in that gallery, we ended the session discussing how his anger is not expressed in his life, but through the compensatory function that expressed itself in the art. It gave him significant insight as to the source of his back pain and nervousness, as he understood that, by encapsulating his anger, he inevitably pays through psychosomatic effects.

K: So it's all about the chronology and the interrelation, the interaction of the characters. How does this internal world of archetypes connect to Expressive Arts Therapy & Coaching?

A: If you remember, we spoke about Mood. If you succeed at creating a Mood atmosphere in Expressive Arts Therapy & Coaching, meaning the client's defense mechanism is reduced, then imagination activates freely, and expressivity is available. This means that there are characters, symbols, a story comes out, there is a lot of imaginative production and the inner world of the client appears on stage. This is the purpose of Expressive Therapies. Stephen Levine (1992) says: "The therapeutic space can become a theater for the presentation of the Self," and later on he claims: "The task of therapy is not to eliminate suffering but to give a voice to it, to find a form in which it can be expressed."

References

Baumann, A. (2005) The Golden Hairs of the Devil. Grimm Fairytails of the Soul's Dark Side. Modan Publishing House, Ben Shemen, Israel.

Campbell, J. (1949) The Hero with a Thousand Faces. Pantheon Books

Furth, G. (1988) The Secret World of Drawings, Healing Through Art. Sigo Press. Boston.

Harari, Y. A Brief History of Mankind (Sapiens), Kinneret, Zmora-Bitan, Dvir Pub. House, Or Yehuda, Israel

Hopcke, R.H (1990) Men's Dreams-Men's Healing. Hebrew: Hakibbutz Hameuhad Pub.

Jung, C.G, Von Franz, M., L. Henderson, J. Jacobi, and A. Jaffe (1964) Man and His Symbols, Picador Published by Pan Book.

Jung, C.G. (1952) Antwort auf Hiob, Hebrew translation: Miriam Kraus & Haim Mahlev, Resling Pub. Tel Aviv.

Jung, C. G. (1971) Psychological Types. Bollingen Series, Princeton.

Jung C.G (2009) The Red Book Liber Novus. Philemon Series. W.W Norton & Company. New York London.

Jung, E. (1974), Animus and Anima, Spring Publications, Zurich.

Levine, S. (1992) Poiesis. The Language of Psychology and the Speech of the Soul. Palmerston Press. Toronto.

Netzer, R. (2011), The Hero Journey, Modan Publishing House, Ben Shemen, Israel.

Neumann, E. (1953) "Mensch und Sinn," in: Hebrew Translation, Psychology Series, Translated Tamar Kron and David Wieler, Resling Pub. , Israel 2013.

Pearson, C. S. (1986) The Hero Within, Six Archetypes We live By, Harper, San Francisco.

Samuels, A. (1986), A Critical Dictionary of Jungian Analysis, Routledge, London & New York.

Sedgwick, D. (1994) The Wounded Healer, Countertransference from a Jungian Perspective. Routledge. London & New York.

Von Franz, M. L (1988) The Way of the Dream. Windrose Films LTD. Toronto.

Whan, M. (1987) Chiron's Wound: Some Reflections on the Wounded Healer, In: Archetypal Processes in Psychotherapy. Chiron Publications.

Chapter 5

Object Relations Applied to Expressive Arts Therapy & Coaching

Object Relations Applied to Expressive Arts Therapy & Coaching

A: This chapter is a kaleidoscope of interwoven concepts, which serves as a quilt for explaining the psychodynamic interactions that take place during the drama of Expressive Arts Therapy and Coaching.

While the chapter on the Creation Axis taught us about the six stages of Expressive Arts Therapy, the chapter about Gestalt explained how to *activate* and *personify* the artistic object, and the Jungian chapter educated us about the *symbolic* meaning of the images which appear in the art itself. This chapter deals with the *relationship* between the creator (client), his artistic object, and the observer (the coach or therapist).

K: What is Object Relations Theory and how does it connect to Expressive Arts Therapies and Coaching?

A: Relationships and attachment start in very early childhood, when we were first exposed to mother-baby relationships. This primal, instinctual, basic parent-baby reciprocity is defined as "Object Relations." Psychoanalysts who followed Freud developed theories based on those crucial, yet fragile relationships. Object Relations Theory suggests that the way people relate to themselves, to others, to situations in their lives, and even to things, is shaped throughout those very early mother (or rather, maternal figure) and baby experiences during infancy. It means, almost, that you are *not* born with a chance to choose to become who you are, and it also means that basic conditions that are crucial to psychic wellbeing (I am not speaking about the physical wellbeing) are imposed on us, in the very beginning of our interaction as babies with our maternal images. You may infer that, during that crucial period, our personality is designed, as well as our psychopathologies.

Before we dive into these intricate theories, I should stress a crucial point: Much more than the actual live care-giver who nurtures the baby or child, and does indeed hold an essential role in shaping his personality, the theories of Object Relations mostly deal with the inner fantasy perceptions which the baby or child holds regarding his significant care-giver. I shall speak about a "Parental Image," about persecution fantasies, megalomaniacal power and castration anxiety.

Melanie Klein's concepts as applied to clinical expressive arts therapies and coaching

Melanie Reizes Klein was an Austrian-British psychoanalyst who devised novel therapeutic techniques for children that influenced child psychology and contemporary psychoanalysis. She was a leading innovator in Object Relations theory. Klein was a disciple of Freud. Her most important contribution to this field lies in the fact that she was very courageous in diving into the baby's mental life, but mostly into the baby's fantasy. Juliet Mitchell, in her book *The Selected Melanie Klein* (1991) explains how Klein "deepened the psychological principles of infant analysis," and arrived at a psycho-analytic play technique with children. R. D. Hinshekwood (1991) registers Klein's 1920 theory about early fantasy activity in the minds of babies. As they cannot report verbally about their fears or desires, Klein's assumptions were only tested later on, and subsequently validated through live observations. Her findings created the theoretical basis for those who followed her. Let me quote Klein herself: "The baby's primitive ego cannot perceive or conceive of the objects in its external world as whole, multifaceted persons. Instead, it lives in a world of one-dimensional objects that have either good or bad intentions towards the infant" (Klein, 1932). This attitude turns the baby as suspicious of the world. Klein (1929) noticed that "the objects were related to as if they had similar single-minded attitudes and impulses towards the ego. Some objects were feared and hated, as terrifyingly violent and punitive, and some were loved for their equal benevolence. The objects themselves had internal states, and the ego was greatly preoccupied by their good or bad relations with itself." This sharply redirected Klein's attention away from the satisfactions of libidinal impulses and toward the relations to objects. The predominance of the child's hatred and fears led Klein (1932), at first, to concentrate on "the harshness of objects," and she believed it represented, in play, a superego of great ferocity.

    According to the Object Relations Theory, the maternal image presents, for the baby, an *"Object,"* and therefore the child is the *"Subject."* Because the two concepts can be confusing, I prefer that all that refers to the mother's repertoire or maternal image (Object) be termed "Parental Image," and what refers to the "Subject" we shall term either child or baby or toddler. We shall soon see how "Object" (mother) and "Subject" (baby) are involved in Expressive Arts Therapies and Coaching.

K: Why Parental? When you call it parental, it means that somebody has a specific role?

A: Parenting is not only breeding and educating. In Object Relations Theory, we learn that the parental image has an important role in shaping the child's personality, especially *the child's internal world*. The parent has many psychological roles which are crucial for the well-being of the child's psyche. So we shall see that the parent, and even more the parent's *internalized image*, are crucial to shaping the child's sense of self, and this includes a provision for the child's psychological needs, for example mirroring the child (meaning reflecting the child's behavior to highlight how they are behaving), nurturing, containing, stimulating and attuning. Object Relations Theory deals with "Relatedness," a concept which denotes the need and ability to have close affectionate relationships with others.

K: How is a Parental Image made? How is it maintained?

A: We have to realize that any human being, really any mammal, is totally dependent, physiologically, on the nursing of the parent. In the first year of our life, we are condemned to death, unless we learn to consume the nurturing system of our Parent. Eventually the parent turns into a *"parental image."* It might not necessarily be the physical breast (even homosexual couples can feed a baby born with a bottle). What does it mean that I am totally dependent upon an external parent? It means that I have to create a relationship through reciprocity. That I have to gain my survival and, in return, perhaps I have to give something back. The basic assumption here is that, because of the vital mutual interrelationship between the parent and the baby, the baby develops an *internal imaginative image*, an internal representation of the nurturing figure, meaning the *parental image*. So there is an actual parent, in reality, who inspires a built-up phantasmal, fictional image of the parent, which gradually integrates with the internal reality of the infant.

When the baby is hungry, all his bodily responses (both physically and emotionally) call for the gratifying Parental Image. This existential need builds up a whole psychic structure of dependency and attachment. We can witness the enthusiasm of the baby and his motivation to be connected, even fuse with the gratifying Parental Image. This dependency is the source of consumption, love, admiration, as well as hate, frustration, possessiveness, competition and rage. This maternal-child dependency system, as in every marketplace, is based on give and take. Because the system is not symmetrical (baby needs Mom much more than Mom needs baby), very often the baby "pays" reluctantly, by giving up on his true needs and by complying with the Parental Image expectations.

K: Yes, this complicated notion of a baby's internal image, how does it possibly connect?

A: Gradually, the baby starts to realize the qualities of this providing system. The first stage is important. This is what Melanie Klein (1946) termed a *Schizo-Paranoid Position*. Schism in Greek means split, cut in two, divided, and paranoid, as you know, is suspicious. This urge to "swallow" the maternal image makes the baby think "Wow, as much as I swallow, I can be swallowed by others." This is where the monster image is created in the fantasy of the baby. It doesn't necessarily need to be a monster, in the traditional sense. It can be a strange person who approaches the child. The baby differentiates the mother, the known object, as a "good breast," and the unknown is potentially a persecutor, labeled by Klein as a "bad breast." This notion that I can "swallow," but I can also be "swallowed," is the source of the Schizo-Paranoid Position (as she termed it).

K: If I understand correctly, Melanie Klein tried to analyze the primer psyche from which the child operates?

A: The child is afraid to be "swallowed," and he develops the Schizo-Paranoid Position, he becomes paranoid, defensive, competitive, strives for the actual concrete target (he wants to have possession of the breast, and accepts nothing symbolic as a replacement—only the breast itself), makes a split between the desired and the aversive, and looks at life from a dichotomous point of view. This Schizo-Paranoid Position is a life experience that can characterize our approach to life in adulthood, as well.

K: And where do Expressive Therapies and Coaching come in?

A: All these traits are totally relevant to Expressive Arts Therapy and Coaching, because people who express themselves through arts, when their predisposition to expressivity is Schizo-Paranoid, their art production, and their response to the art they produced, is characterized by suspicion and fear. They are afraid to let go in the Improvisation phase of the Creation Axis. They rationalize, make concrete art, and avoid distancing to the level of symbolic experience. They are not original, and they produce what they think is expected, what is common, and they are far from authentic in their creativity.

Let's keep in mind that Expressive Therapies revert backwards to this pre-verbal Schizo-Paranoid developmental stage. When you make art, you do not use words. The non-verbal expression associates the client with his early childhood in the cradle, where he corresponded emotionally with his Parental Images without words. In early childhood, by screaming, smiling, caressing, crawling, waving, and using facial and body gestures, the infant actually uses the repertoire of Expressive Arts Therapies to communicate.

The Schizo-Paranoid Position is quite challenging for the parent, because the child is not easy with strangers, and is obsessively possessive of private objects and toys. There is a whole repertoire of responses and artistic productions typical of the Schizo-Paranoid predisposition. All our mistrustful clients who come to therapy or coaching in the Schizo-Paranoid Position need first

Object Relations Applied to Expressive Arts Therapy & Coaching

to establish trust.[1] Not only trust towards the therapist and the method, but also trust throughout the Creation Axis, suspicion towards the media, and the possible damage it may cause. "Can I clean this color stain in the laundry?" they ask. "How do you expect me to work with clay? This is done in kindergarten." They are ambivalent in the expressive experience, and create a split. A split between the client and the therapist, and ambivalence within the client himself. "One side of me wants to, but the other doesn't," they confess. They are torn over the art materials: "It is attracting me, but nevertheless disgusts me." This split prevails on all levels of relationships, between the client and the Parental Image, between client and himself, between the client and the artistic object. Also, the person is very critical, hesitating to let go of his defenses. In this phase, the client is not generous with himself, without compassion, and is busy with little details, instead of trusting the process.

K: How do you help the client move away from this Schizo-Paranoid trap?

A: Here is the magic: If you succeed in persuading the client to let his art production talk to him then, by letting the art speak to the client, we have a chance to cure the client, and shift him out from the Schizo-Paranoid Position to the *Depressive Position*, which is the position where he can really enjoy relationships and art. This is because the artwork knows how to soften the client's Schizo-Paranoid attitude. The artistic product possesses psychological qualities such as humbleness,

---

1 See Chapter 1 on Trust

modesty, gratefulness and innocence. Once they are uttered, the client is usually surprised, and cherishes his own humanistic assets, spoken out from within the created art.

K: So, what is the second phase? What is this *Depressive Position*? How is it created?

A: I keep on stressing that there is a constant learning function that takes place in the human relationship and experience. We are learning all the time. Here, too, the child gradually learns that, although he is very fearful, and although there is a threat, apparently the threatening object does not actually execute him, swallow him, as it is solely a part of his own imaginative inner reality. He begins to understand that these are his subjective fears. It is easy for him to get away from the fears, to ignore them, and to lean more on the gratifying gestures of his nurturing Parental Image. Through exploration and experience, the child eventually understands that his inner reality is a distortion of the actual external reality. He uses machanisms of difenses such as split and projective idenifictation to cope with reality. This delusion (swallowing the Parental Image and consequently being swallowed) is an illusion. When the delusion starts presenting in the child's psyche, he starts straying away from the Schizo-Paranoid Position, surrendering to the Depressive Position. The child passes from split approach into the perception of the desired object (Parental Image) as a whole. You may be surprised that a Depressive Position is, paradoxically, a positive and recommended life experience. You must keep in mind that Klein's "Depressive Position" is not the clinical depression you know from psychopathology. Depression here refers to "mood," to withdrawal and humility.

K: How does the baby come up with this idea?

A: Because, realistically, nobody causes him harm, he can gradually accept substitutes for the Parental Image, and develop a cohesive self and an integrated ego. The child shifts from the concrete need to the symbolic compromising stanza. By realizing this, he is withdrawing into the position Melanie Klein calls the *Depressive Position*. The child learns that his grandiose fantasy about omnipotence is just an illusion. This is causing, on the positive side, a sense of collaboration. In order to collaborate, you have to look at things symbolically. I want something concrete, but I cannot get it, so I have to distance and generalize and see that the alternative is just as comforting. I can withdraw and give up on my original desire. Because the substitute is as good as the desired original fantasy, I can collaborate and, on a higher level, look at life from a symbolic point of view.

In Expressive Arts Therapies and Coaching, this is a preliminary condition for a successful process. Dealing with arts and performing requires symbolic comprehension. The symbolic aspect of the artistic experience enables the client to flow with the process because, by stepping away from a certain issue and generalizing it, one allows oneself to see what is in common with this particular wound. We must be able to distance and see how it presents itself in the artistic here and now, from aesthetic distancing, and how it has to do with other issues that center around the same category, meaning that it is essential to arrive at a new adaptive approach.

K: Is this related to the Gestalt principle that "the whole is greater than the sum of its parts?"

A: Yes, bravo. The creation, the redesigning, reframing the problem, looking at it from different aspects, enables the client to shift and move and change. A key word in the Depressive Position is "Relativity." Relativity means that, although the desired is not what I want, I can accept it reluctantly, as the symbolic is as good as the original.

K: This Depressive Position seems a really significant state to achieve. Where and how can I bring the client to it, in Expressive Arts Therapies and Coaching?

A: It is a natural development that most children pass through when they benefit from "good enough parenthood" (in Winnicott's terms). When the client creates an artwork, starts playing or flows into movement, in the Improvisation phase, he will inevitably make mistakes, as he is adapting to the media, trying to express an idea, actualize it. There will always be a discrepancy between what the client intended to do, and what his artistic process yielded. If he is in a Schizo-Paranoid position, he will not accept the outcome, and will look at it with despair or disdain. He will criticize it: "It's totally not what I had expected." Just like a mother saying: "I had a beautiful dream about my son, but this son does not fit my expectations." In the

Depressive Position, the client can accept the outcome lovingly, not because it is so precious for its objective values, but because this is subjectively his. This is an approach that demonstrates compassion, acceptance and compromise, which nurtures the artistic results.

Let's look at a little baby sculpture a client has just made out of clay, which symbolizes his vulnerability.

She says: "This baby is vulnerable and helpless." If you cannot arrive at symbolization, and understand what that art product is signifying, what meanings it brings you, what the added value of this concrete image is, you will stay on the artistic level of technical gratification, perhaps, yet be unable to take a step further, a step deeper into the symbolic meaning, which will finally reveal the secret underlying it. For this, you have to approach through the Depressive Position, to be in touch with your own wound.

K: So, it is a moment of realization, when you get in touch with the reality that is not according to my expectations, my anticipated results, but at the same time to accept it, to comply with the outcome?

A: Yes, so whenever the client says: "But this art is less exciting than the one I did last week," he approaches the experience from the Schizo-Paranoid point of view, but if he says:" This one is different, yet I like it anyway," he looks at life from the Depressive Position.

K: When, in what stage, does the client move into the Depressive Position? How can the therapist help him move into the Depressive Position?

A: Your question is leading me to the essence of the Expressive Arts therapeutic experience, which is the dialogue with the art that one made. Talk to it, and be courageous in granting your art autonomy. Let it expose wisdom from the within. It means that the therapist has to help the client step out of the Schizo-Paranoid, narcissistic and egocentric pole, and allow the art product to speak in the I-Thou technique, letting the art own its truth, bringing out psychic contents which are projected from the art itself.

My clinical and teaching work has taught me that people blocked by a defense mechanism point of view try to avoid letting themselves go, from diving into their own artistic works. I see inevitable obstacles when Expressive Therapists prefer to speak with the client about the artwork, about motivation and associations but, while doing this, they stay on the first three levels of meaning, and do not encourage the release of the Secret.

K: What you're saying is that a client comes with a problem, a wound, made in early childhood, that keeps repeating. He comes with this wound in the Schizo-Paranoid Position. When you begin to uncover the fourth level of meaning, the Secret, you can shift your client to the Depressive Position. The subject, the client, gets over his fear of being "swallowed" by this scar, and learns to accept it, which leads to change or remission of the problem. Did I understand correctly?

A: Wonderful! It is always amazing to witness a client shifting, in the presence of his or her own artwork, from the Schizo-Paranoid Position to the Depressive Position, where their whole attitude turns from persecution into compassion. We have, by now, an artistic product. I spoke about the artistic product having its own autonomy, speaking directly to the client. This artistic product will not necessarily tell the client something that will fit his expectations. At this point, when you encourage and enable relatedness between the client and the artistic product, you present the client with the chance to shift from Schizo-Paranoid to Depressive Positions. The moment the therapist enabled your artistic product to talk, the moment you started the dialogue between yourself and your own artistic product, relatedness begins between the client and the art product. *This relatedness is a duplication of a Parental Image (client) – Child (artistic product) dialogue.*

K: This is exciting. Can you further elaborate on the relevance to Expressive Arts Therapies?

A: I claim that the artistic productions, made and performed by our clients, in the course of Expressive Arts Therapies, can serve as a rehabilitating stage in the baby-Parental Image relationships, which perhaps had been damaged in our clients' early stages of life. It does not necessarily relate to the mother-child history, it can be a father perhaps, some authority from the client's childhood, or even a problematic or malfunctioning personality, which developed as a result of early traumas with which the client needs to deal in adulthood.

Our psyche is analogous to an internal theater. There is a whole theater that, through Expressive Arts Therapies, can be projected through artistic stimulants onto the external world. By projecting this internal theater, from the inside out, we have a chance, in Expressive Arts Therapies, to shape and cure our psychological wounds. Psychodynamic theories assume that one can cure the client's narcissistic wound through playful interactions. This is where Klein invented the box play therapy. I think that Expressive Arts Therapy's added value (based on psychoanalytic principles) is a very efficient method, because it reconstructs the maternal-baby primer relationships through authentic experiences similar to our early childhood, mostly during the pre-verbal stage (meaning, before language has even been developed). In Expressive Arts Therapies, the Parental Image can be considered any artistic product (drawing, dancing, singing, acting) which reflects the internal psyche of the client. *Please do note this amazing paradox: Although the client has created the artifact, once the artifact is granted autonomy and allowed to talk to its creator, the roles capsizes! The creator (client) becomes the baby-child and the artifact turns into the Parental Image role. This is why the I-Thou technique is so effective.*

Who are the actors on the Expressive Art Therapies theatrical stage? The plastic arts, the movement, music with which the client builds creative relationships. When you put all three in performing arts, you create a theatrical drama. These actors (the drama, the music, the movement, the dance, the poetry, the plastic arts, the paintings and sculptures) are all products which our clients created, invested with intention, loved, surely cared about, so obviously they established a certain attachment to those artifacts, which derived from their creativity and imagination (internal resources). By this, we reestablish the relationship between two parties– the artist (the client in a mother role) and his artistic production (in a baby role). However, when the artifact is allowed to speak up, it turns the roles upside-down and, as I explained, the creator (client) turns into the baby-child, and the artifact, indeed, turns into the Parental image. Because Object Relations Theory deals deeply with the psychodynamic factors in relationships, it explains the relationships between the client and his artistic productions, which are analogous to Parental-Child experiences. Here lies a chance for cure and alter narcissistic scars through the artistic process.

The client manifests either sadism, antipathy or detachment towards his artistic production, or may totally connect, narcissistically invest, lovingly impressed by his artistic production. At the same time, he may convey his expectation of the observer (the therapist or coach) to be impressed by his artistic maneuvers, wishing to be mirrored (in the Object Relations sense). There is a whole bunch of relationship issues which interweave in a creative artistic process. All we learned about object relations occurs along the Creation Axis.

K: So, what you're saying is that Object Relations Theory is such that it can express itself through arts?

A: Indeed. We are looking at what was produced in the arts which reflects the client's object relations patterns, complexes, wounds and disturbances. What does the personified (Gestalt I-Thou) sculpture (child) feel or say to the artist (client) who created it? What does the crazy movement around the room say to the runner? What does this sweet melody say to the person who plays it? By personifying the artistic production, by granting the art momentary autonomy to speak for itself, as an inborn autonomous creation, we can reconstruct the client's interrelationship life story. By taking this point of view, you give autonomy to the artistic image, and you enable the art, music, movement to speak for itself and maybe also, as all children do, to complain about the Parental Image, the artist, the dancer, musician who produced those artifacts. And, at the same time, roles can be shifted and, paradoxically, the artifact can turn into a Parental Image for the client, and correct the client's attitude into an empathic approach.

    Taking this relationship from the paradoxical point of view of the produced artistic output, and not from the narcissistic point of view of the creator, shows that you understand the healing power of the artistic product.

K: Who followed Klein, and what are the continuing theories that accompany you in applying Object Relations to Expressive Arts Therapies and Coaching?

Donald Winnicott's concepts as applied to clinical expressive arts therapies and coaching

Donald Woods Winnicott was an English pediatrician and psychoanalyst who was especially influential in the field of Object Relations Theory. Winnicott (1960) coined the concepts of *True and False Selves*. Following Winnicott, one of the biggest contributions, which Alice Miller (1979) taught us in her book *The Drama of the Gifted Child,* is that in a False Self situation, the child gives up on his authentic personality, and shapes himself according to the parent's expectations. As if the baby says to himself: "I will give up on my True Self and my genuine belief, my character, my natural instincts, my wish, in order to obtain love and acceptance." Donald Winnicott (1966) defined for us what is a *"good enough" parent.* He claimed that "an idealized parent is a provider who is attuned not only to the physiological provision of the child, but even more to the psycho-emotional needs of the child." Now this is a very big obstacle, and my 40 years of experience show that it is a risk and an option that can result in a huge scar. Unfortunately, most biological parents don't go to school in order to become certified "good enough" parents.

To sum up this part of my explanation, let me present to you with a short vignette.

I was asked to consult to a mother about her six-year-old daughter, whose hair was falling out. She was not pulling it out, which is a known psychopathology (Trichotillomania). It is simply drops out. Immediately, I asked her: "Is there a father in the picture?" She replied no, as she raised the child alone. The mother was confused, because it was hard for her to admit to me that the biological father had been sent away by her, right after the girl was born. She was arrogant, tough and said to her man, "You are not the right person to raise our daughter," and she erased him from her daughter's life. By the age of six, this girl was totally dependent on a tyrannical maternal system. This woman, who'd kicked out her husband, is very strict with tough superego, and the girl has apparently developed a persecuting internal mother image and is afraid to oppose her . Had she opposed her only parental figure she would have either become psychotic, or needed to comply totally with her mother. Mom said that she was a very obedient, satisfactory child, of course. Finally, at the age of six, somebody recommended that the mother tell the girl the story of her biological father. By then, the mother had another partner in life. The moment the mother told the girl that there was a biological father somewhere, the mother misbalanced the mental equilibrium that had existed since the girl was born. Before, she'd been the only Parental Image, and now the girl, in her imagination, created an idealized father. She started to fantasize about him, and the moment she connected to this potential father image, this father became an existing internal object for her. She would go into the streets and ask herself: "Is this my father? Is this my father?" She kept, in her imagination, a catalogue of potential fathers. You may ask me why her hair fell out? My assumption is based on Esther Bick (1968). She claims, in her article about the "secondary skin," that our skin is a substitute for our parental hugging wrap. Every skin problem, allergy or wound, scars that do not heal, may be related, psychosomatically, to empathic failures of the Parental Image. The break in that girl's "parental wrap" (to use Bick's terminology) might have manifested in the hair loss. Now, I expect you to ask me what this story has to do with Clinical Expressive Arts Therapy and soon I shall tell you about the girl's therapeutic intervention I did.

K: Which concepts by Winnicott are applied by you in Clinical Expressive Therapy and Coaching, then?

A: Donald Winnicott brings several concepts which deepen our understanding of the artistic process. Winnicott himself was a very creative scholar, and his theory is impressive in its original concepts, for example the False and True Selves.

K: Which are the two sorts of Selves, according to Winnicott?

A: Davis & Wallbridge (1981), in their chapter "The False Self," describe what Winnicott (1960) wrote about the development of the child's True Self and False Self. Those two concepts I find very relevant to Expressive Therapies. In order to explain how the True Self and the False Self develop, I usually give an example about a young mother who is studying and is terribly invested in her academic career, but at the same time (as happens often these days), she has also become a mother. By now, she has a four-month-old baby, but she needs to study for the final exam. She wants to be efficient. Efficiency is one of these obstacles that parents fall into, and sacrifice the True Self of their child in hopes of achieving it. Because they want to be efficient, they will eventually raise a child with a False Self, who will be compliant. This young student mother wants to nurse the child and even breastfeed. When she is sure he is done, and puts him to bed, he starts crying, so she feeds him from the other breast, and puts him in bed. Yet the baby cries again, so she picks him up. She concludes from this cry that he is still hungry, goes to the kitchen and makes him extra formula. At this point, the baby is located in what I termed the "T situation:" A point from which the baby cannot go further, he cannot keep on crying. If he keeps on crying, he will turn blue, he may start vomiting, and his Self will be disturbed. So, the baby needs to make a decision, either comply with his Mom and develop a False Self, as he doesn't want to eat anymore, actually he wants to play with Mom, or he can believe he is still hungry, consume the extra food offered to him and calm down. There is a hidden contract here, where the baby supposedly says, "I will give up on playing now and, in return, I will be your beloved child, you will put me asleep." A colleague of hers, who studies with her, will soon come. She will be proud of her angelic baby, who fell asleep and allowed her to study. This False Self helped the infant adapt, assimilate and accommodate to his mother's expectation. The mother and child are in harmony, but the price is that the child has developed a False Self.

However, let's observe the other direction of the

T situation. The other option is that the child is very intelligent, that he ate enough, he slept enough, and he wanted to play with Mommy. This is his True Self: He wanted attention and love. If mother was less efficient, she could have kept him awake, study with her friend and, once the child fell asleep, put him in bed. By this, she would have confirmed and respected his True Self. But obviously the price might be that she would study less.

K: What does this have to do with Expressive Arts Therapies and Coaching?

A: The art usually reveals not only the truth and desires, but also is the product of spontaneity of the True Self. When people perform, the natural creative axis usually reveals one's True Self. As Expressive Therapists, we have to look for those true, authentic artistic products. However, often we see a person who dances a too-labored dance, supposing an imitation that complies with a culture or style. The body movements are too forced, or we may observe a client approaching the art buffet and he grabs tremendous amounts of art materials—these might be hinting at False Self artistic behavior. You see that the art materials taken from the buffet are later used just for the sake of decoration, impersonation and denying depth. If you hear cacophony, over-loud music, and you cannot really feel how the person is connected to it, it might be a sign of False Self. Such music is dictated by external criteria, and does not derive from an authentic connectedness.

To differentiate between a False and an authentic artifact, one is required to use differential diagnosis. Differential diagnosis is the distinguishing of a particular disease or condition from others that present similar clinical features. There are two ways to check whether the artistic act is False or True. One, which is most recommended, is to ask the client: "What did this movement mean to you?" You can even go into details, "What did this ankle twisting dance move mean to you?" Diagnose the movement and encourage the client simply to give explanations for what this meant to him, and how he associates with it. If we go to the levels of meaning (as in Chapter One), these questions lead to the "simple" level. If we head towards the interpretative level of meaning, the expressive therapist needs to be professionally acquainted with the medias he's working with, in order to spot clues which will validate a false versus authentic style. When the client is performing, you want to be able to analyze the movement process. If you observe a discrepancy between what you know about the dilemma that your client is trying to express, or what you know about the client's character, and what is manifested, very likely the expression is false.

However, sometimes it's complicated. Sometimes the True Self is totally not aesthetic. Sometimes the True Self conveys "to hell with all this beauty," and it seems, from an outside perspective, chaotic or tough. You might say that the client does not invest himself, but this is not true. Our only assurance is a dialogue with the client. But if we don't have in mind that there are two sorts of artistic styles, true and false, we will not look for precise indications.

K: If the therapist brings to the client's awareness his false approach, are you sure this will cure the client's false tendency?

A: No, because there is another concept of Winnicott's which is relevant to the move from False into True Self. The concept is "the Destruction of the Object."

The baby needs to be provided with physical conditions, and soon learns to demand his needs. He sees the Paternal Image as a functioning mechanism. I will scream, and you will provide for me. Operating on the parent is not only a real-life experience, claims Winnicott, it is also an inner imaginative constellation, the baby-child really imagines and believes he can destroy the parent. Before age three, the Self is integrated. By this age, the child differentiates between mother and father, and senses his gender identify, capable now of talking, communicating and moving about. By the age of three, he has developed a functional self and, naturally, he is egocentric and a functional organism. How can we expect such an egocentric creation to turn into a considerate personality, expecting him to see the other, not through his needy eyes, but from the perspective of the other. This is almost a metamorphosis, to change an egocentric mechanism into a merciful, compassionate, providing human being. Actually, we are back into the issue of shifting from Schizo-Paranoid into Depressive Position.

For this personality transformation, Winnicott (1971) in his book, *Playing and Reality,* coined the concept of "Destruction of the Object."

I shall translate for you Winnicott's idea into a simple version. Winnicott claims that, in order for the toddler to move from his egocentric position into a considerate position, the toddler needs to try to destroy the parent, and if the parent tolerates the destructing attempts, only then can the child shift successfully into the upgraded mature position of considerate and collaborative relationships. Winnicott uses two crucial concepts which form two stages of development. The first stage is labelled: "Relate to the Object." This means that the child consumes the parent as a functional organism. The child sees the parent as a provider who is out there to fulfill his narcissistic desires. It is expected that, after the child passes a transitional phase where he or she tries to destroy the parent, if the parent survives the attacks, the child will eventually move into the phase which Winnicott termed "Using the object."

K: What does it mean "Destroying an Object?"

A: I think that the inevitable need and dependency of the child upon the parent's provisions, and the cost of giving up on his True Self by complying to the parent and yielding to a False Self which satisfies the precious parent, all cause the child to become self-centered and egocentric. At a certain point, the parent expects the child to see him or her as a human being, with vulnerabilities and needs, as well. The child checks borders, attempts to negate the idealized parent, provokes and rebels him or her. These attempts to break the parent are called "Destruction of the Object." The crucial point here is that, if the parent survives those attempts, meaning that she or he does not sadistically punish the child nor humiliate him, only then can the child realize the parent's realistic status, and then the child can move on to the mature position of "Using the object," meaning building up benign reciprocal relationships.

K: And how does all this connect to Expressive Arts Therapies?

A: The infant needs to try to destroy the Parental Image. Children and adolescents who are referred to therapy sometimes enter therapy not because of the reported, manifested symptoms, but rather because of failure in the developmental process, not being able to pass from Relating to the Object to Using the Object.

Adults and children, in therapy or coaching, expect us to improve their capacity for Relatedness. As Expressive Therapists, we have to try not to allow the object (including ourselves) to be destroyed. Much emphasis has to be put on the client's approach to the artistic product. How do you relate to what you have just performed? Take note of how the client perceives the therapist's role in the session. Does the therapist turn into a partner, a servant or an object to annoy or harass? Notice what type of relational attitude is projected by the client onto the object, as is manifested in his stories, sculptures, paintings, songs and movement.

For example, in a movement session, if the client is brutal, jumping and at risk of breaking his leg, making very risky movements, this means that he is destroying himself. Notice the type of relational attitude in his stories, sculptures, paintings, and try to intervene by the attempt to change the relating attitude to the object into the Winnicottian sense. For example, the art therapist should say: "Do you think this black needs these white spots now?" Or: "Do you think this sculpture really needs to be shaped so tightly, because it might bend and break?" We are dealing here with the question of how one can self-maintain wide, reciprocal and fruitful relationships with real other selves (people), who exist beyond one's internal imaginative world. It is about experiencing such relationships without feeling threatened by the difference of the other, without feeling intruded on or helpless in the presence of separateness and otherness. How can we enjoy the other's truthful selfness, if not on account of our own selfness? How can we deeply accept the existence of another subject, its right to express itself and even accept its impact, "using" the other (as Winnicott defines it) in order to refill ourselves with a substance which is not "Me" and, at the same time, not feel less special, less central, and without being shaken? How to arrive at the "I-Thou" relationship, in Martin Buber's terms?

K: Please go on telling me how all this expresses itself in the performing sessions.

A: While watching a client at work, I am impressed by how he uses to his artistic product. How he nurtures it. How he wants to smooth the clay, spontaneously pulling saliva from his mouth and caressing and brushing or soothing the clay, regressing to a very primal act. Or if a student needs to take a break and leaves his work on the floor, asking a nearby student to take care of it. Or in the Preservation phase at the end of the Creation Axis, the client will ask where we are going to keep the work, will smooth it, and would like it to be on the shelf, not at the edge of the shelf, to be safe or possibly hidden. How a client learns to "use" the object, be it his artifact, his friends or the environment.

K: Can you give me an example of a client who, through the Destruction of the Object, came to accept the object's actuality and sustainability?

A: It is quite easy to observe this process while working with Jungian sand trays with young children (age 4 - 10). Often you can see those children create a split: gather two opposing groups, or two antagonistic heroes, or one victimized hero and the opposition is the child himself. The Main Theme is an endless sadistic scene of hurting, torturing, burying, killing or tearing apart one side. Gradually, after a long time of destroying the object (which obviously sustains the disastrous treatment), a striking and abrupt change appears. You can notice a gesture of compassion, reconciliation and finally negotiations displayed, which bring a new culture of collaboration. I always feel relief when this change finally occurs, the child learns to use the object. Now we are ready to create a peaceful scene featuring benign conflicts and challenges. If the client can accept this artwork as representative of the here and now that he has to commit to, investigate and nurture, then it means that the client has accessed the Depressive Position.

K: You're mentioning Relatedness as a fundamental condition for a cure. I think you mean certain Relatedness. What is it?

A: What I mean by Relatedness is how you lay out your intentions in the presence of the significant other. It can also be an object. I'll give you an example: Children in therapy sometimes use the art and its facilities in a very egocentric manner. They can be dirty, break tools, they can be very enthusiastic about what they do and, when their parent comes pick them up, they leave you, the room and their artistic product as if a storm passed by. No Relatedness. This is why I stress the importance of the Preservation phase in the Creation Axis. By passing the door threshold, we're obliged to pay attention the child's object relatedness.

K: Who followed Winnicott?

A: This is the point where I have to present to you Thomas Ogden's (1989) concept of the "Primitive Edge of Experience." Upon birth, during the pre-verbal stage the child communicates with the parental images through his senses. The non-lingual baby can communicate only through the following channels: He can scream, laugh, utter sounds, he can move his legs and hands, gently or hectically. He can soil himself or urinate, and this is how he operates on the environment. The baby transfers his intentions to the parental figure through his senses. As a result, although the parental figure can talk and translate those non-verbal gestures into words, as Daniel Stern (1905) explains, the parental image also responds through his or her sensational repertoire (cradling, soothing, lifting, whispering, singing, hushing, etc.) This very early phase of communication through the senses was called, by Ogden, the "Primitive Edge of Experience."

If you accumulate all of these non-verbal sensational gestures, you arrive at the domain of Expressive Arts Therapies.

K: I realized that you failed to keep up with the term "Parental Image," and frequently called it simply the Mother or maternal figure.

Wilfrid Bion – four functions of the mother's role and its applications in clinical expressive arts therapies and coaching

A: Wilfred Bion was an influential British psychoanalyst, who became president of the British Psychoanalytical Society from 1962 to 1965. He was a potent and original contributor to psychoanalysis. We ask ourselves what is the mother's role, or how can an art product, made in Expressive Therapy, turn into a "Parental Image" for the client? For this, we have to turn to W. R. Bion.

Hani Biran (2015), in her book *The Courage of Simplicity: Essential Ideas in the Work of W. R. Bion*, explains the four functions of the mother's role. Let's check whether the personified artistic product can function as a mother's role. Bion defines the maternal figure. *Please pay attention: Not mother, but Maternal Figure. This means that any artistic product can function as a figure, if it possesses maternal qualities.*

A Maternal Figure according to W. Bion is -

An **Active Container** which functions as:
- 1. Translate "Unthinkable thoughts" into acts
- 2. Provide capacity for Reverie: transmit optimism
- 3. Help create an Internal container
- 4. Give "Words" which create "shape"
- 5. Train as a social member, part of "Establishment"

K: So, it manifests as a Parental Image?

A: Yes, it contains the psychological functions of the Parental Image. The first function of the maternal figure is to *translate unthinkable thoughts into acts*. Let's see how this manifests in Expressive Arts Therapies. Whenever you are intrigued with the artistic assignment of assembling pictures from magazines into a collage, once committed to your collection and organizing the outcome so that it displays a narrative or meaning to you, and if you were asked "how is this message connected to your life," it is very possible that the conclusion will lead you to acting or fulfilling what had been expressed in the collage.

To demonstrate this experience, for the sake of the example, let's choose Rita, a single thirty year-old client, she hovers over the visual images, picks up associatively what catches her eyes and picked up the following photos: A Mercedes, a diamond ring, a palace near a lake, and a happy family running along the beach. Rita later arranged the pictures in a circle and wrote "la dolce vita=sweet life". The art transformed for her unthinkable thoughts into a message. She exposed her materialistic approach to life. Rita discusses with me the reason she came to therapy, as she is desperate to have a boyfriend and start a family, yet the collage denotes she is too enchanted by status and external fancy glimmering objects which may cause an obstacle in the process of creating truthful intimate relationship.

In the second function of the mother's role, I check whether the art product can become a maternal figure, *providing capacity for Reverie (Bion's term) and the transmission of optimism.* Reverie is Bion's concept of a maternal "reverie" capacity, and it is based on Klein's assumption of the infant's immature psyche. It refers to the capacity of the maternal image to sense (and make sense of) what is going on inside the infant. The infant does not have a logical mindset, and his psychic existence is imaginary and non-rational, so he needs the maternal figure to shift him gradually to a realistic approach to life. Bion used two terms for this shift: Moving from "Alpha functioning," a dream-like level, *reverie* in French, to "Beta-functioning," which is reasoning and a rational mental adult way of experience.

For example, any artistic process has, in itself, an Alpha functioning experience. It includes playfulness and fantasy, thus it is a Reverie, a dream-like situation. When we bring the dramatic experience down to earth by asking how you connect this experience to your life, or what insight this act grants you, we shift our client to the Beta functioning level.

The third function is to *help create an internal container.* This is a great paradox. Arts are agents of our internal world. The more art we produce, the larger our inner world's container becomes. The client is exposed to a whole repertoire of internal images and contains them in his therapeutic experience.

The fourth function that represents the maternal figure deals with *giving wording, a vocabulary repertoire, which creates "shape."* This job mostly is done by the therapist who observes the dramatic art experience. The therapist gives words, which later will grant the client the ability to shape his behavior and arrive at change. To remind you of the Preservation phase, the last stage of the Creation Axis, after the client arrives at the Main Theme, he can summarize the experience in words, and this articulation will create change. The conclusion of this dramatic experience, made by the therapist and the client, naturally leads to the question "Let's see how this connects to your life" or "Let's summarize what we did today in our session." This is what Bion meant, bringing "Words" into a created "Shape."

Daniel Stern's concepts as applied to clinical expressive arts therapies and coaching

Daniel N. Stern was a prominent American psychiatrist and psychoanalytic theorist, specializing in infant development, on which he had written a number of books — most notably *The Interpersonal World of the Infant*.

K: This mother's role must be an extremely sophisticated talent; no wonder the parental figure often fails to fulfill those four tasks. Are there more challenges facing the maternal image?

A: Yes. Daniel Stern (1985) observed the baby- mother

interactions. His theory of the Self is based on his assumption of the Unity of the Senses. He argues that "philosophy, psychology, and art have a long history of designating shape, time, and intensity to be amodal qualities of experience (in psychological terms) or primary qualities of experience (in philosophical terms)."

Aristotle first postulated a doctrine of sensory correspondence, or a doctrine of the Unity of the Senses. His sixth sense, common sense, was the sense that could apperceive the qualities of sensation that are primary (that is, amodal), in that they do not belong exclusively to any one sense alone, as color belongs to vision, but are shared by all the senses. Psychologists were probably first drawn to the issue of the Unity of the Senses by the phenomenon of synesthesia, in which stimulation in a single sense evokes sensations that belong to a different modality.

Stern published his ideas about the pre-verbal self against the theoretical background of Mahler's theory (1975) regarding the "Psychological Birth of the Human Infant." This theory, dealing with developmental sub-phases, beginning with "the normal autistic phase," continuing with "the beginning of the symbiotic phase" etc., were generally accepted. He also had to cope with the pillars of Kohut's theory concerning the archaic self.

It must have required much intellectual integrity and courage for Stern to follow the findings of his research and arrive at the conclusion that "there is no symbiotic-like phase. In fact, the subjective experiences of union with another can occur only after a sense of a core self and a core other exists." His basic assumption is "that some senses of the Self do exist, long prior to self-awareness and language. These include the senses of agency, of physical cohesion, of continuity in time, of having intentions in mind, and other such experiences... If we assume (he claims) that some preverbal senses of the Self start to form at birth (if not before), while others require the maturation of later-appearing capacities, before they can emerge, then we are freed from the partially semantic task of choosing criteria to decide when a sense of self really begins."

Stern talks about "a sense of the Self which is not a cognitive construct." It begins with the sense of a core Self, which forms the foundation of all the more elaborate senses of the Self that come later. Stern first described seven senses of the Self: The sense of agency, the sense of physical cohesion, the sense of continuity, the sense of affectivity, the sense of a subjective Self that can achieve intersubjectivity with another, the sense of creating organization and the sense of transmitting meaning."

In constructing a developmental path for the sense of the Self, Stern describes four stages, each one defining a different domain of self-experience and social relatedness. "These senses of Self are not viewed as successive phases that replace one another. Once formed, each sense of Self remains fully functioning and active throughout life. All continue to grow and coexist."

In each domain, he formulates crucial concepts, which I intend to explain in detail: First, the sense of an *emergent self,* developing between the time of birth and the age of two months. Here he uses the concepts of *Amodal Perception and Vitality Affects.*

Each one of these concepts has direct relevance to how we relate to the Self issues in Expressive Therapy, and how the arts that we create can rehabilitate and enable the client to restore and reconnect to his inner knowledge, pride, dignity and authentic feelings, which molds him to become a decisive, secure person with definite targets for himself. For me, Self Psychology finally must turn into a practical internal operational system to which the client can connect.

According to Stern, the mother or the Parental Image is corresponding with the baby (before the baby establishes a language) through what he calls *Affect Attunement*. He observed how the baby demonstrates feelings to the parent. Apparently, the preverbal infant transmits affection by *intentional communication*. Through eye contact, through increasing signals, like the voice, shouting, crying, laughing and through changes in the form of signals, whether they are low or high pitched. It's the building of Relatedness through the senses. This obviously reminds us of Ogden's concept of the Primitive Edge of Experience, which we mentioned previously. According to Stern, the Parental Image communicates with the preverbal infant by her spontaneous response to the baby. She may respond in the same *modality* as the child. For example, he is moving and she is moving in return, he is shouting and she hums, he is singing and she is sings. She can moderate between high pitch, low pitch, high and low volume, length and so on.

The phenomena of Affective Attunement of an Intermodal Expressive Therapist would appear to be his capacity for mastering and expressing himself naturally in several modalities. He can take the experience of emotional resonance and automatically recast that experience into another form of expression.

Since Stern (1985) attributes this ability to any normal intuitive mother, I am sure that, to some degree, every Art, Movement and Music Therapist conveys Affective Attunement spontaneously. This happens when the Movement Therapist suddenly claps his hands in unison rhythms, while a claient is moving; or an Art Therapist moves his neck spontaneously up and down, while the patient is drawing a fluctuating line; or the Music Therapist conducts a client's melody in the air with his hands. One should notice that, as the client has his own unique manner of response to the therapist, so, too, Stern points out, the baby communicates affectively with the mother through *"intentional communication."*

This phenomenon often manifests in the Intermodal Expressive therapeutic processes. We are talking about an intense, dramatic, non-verbal activity (even if this takes place within the client –therapist couple), that is characterized by movements, sounds and visual art performance. The client needs to communicate with the therapist, and the most effective manner will be through Intentional Communication. They will express aversion, satisfaction, fear, or eagerness through eye contact, increasing signals, and changes in the form of those signals. These will be absorbed by the therapist and will significantly deepen the emotional relationship between the two.

K: Aren't you talking about mirroring?

A: Yes, Affect Attunement is a sort of mirroring. Affect Attunement is a spontaneous capability of the mother/therapist to be in harmony, and it is shaping the significant other through a harmonious relationship, through the senses.

Daniel Stern (1985) discovers something amazing about the baby's potential. He named it *Amodal Perception*. In clarifying his ideas about the emergent self, Stern argues that there are "three processes involved in forming a sense of an emergent self: Amodal Perception, Physiognomic Perception, and the perception of corresponding Vitality Affects. Stern maintains that it is necessary to formulate new concepts as "many qualities of feeling that occur do not fit into our existing lexicon or taxonomy of affects. These elusive qualities are better captured by dynamic, kinetic terms, such as "surging," "fading away," "fleeting," "explosive," "crescendo," "decrescendo," "bursting," "drawn out," and so on.

Amodal Perception is the child-innate perceptive ability to grasp the world in a holistic intermodal sensational form. By way of Amodal Perception, the baby takes information, receives it in one sensory modality and somehow translates it into another sensory modality. For example, he hears the mother and he is moving his legs. Legs denote kinesthetic movement. How does he know that, when she makes a noise, he is expected to move? How does he transmit the voice from low to high, tuned to the function of his mother's similar kinesthetic movement? He communicates with the mother and, by doing this, he also monitors the mother. If he starts moving his legs quickly, the mother can attune and accelerate her voice. So by using this capacity, the preverbal baby transports a metaphorical feeling to the other. Stern labels this metaphorical transmission *Vitality Affect*. Vitality Affect acts as the supra-modal currency into which stimulation, in any modality, can be translated. This is a kind of Amodal Perception, too, since an affect experience is not bound to any one modality of perception.

    A beautiful example of the way Vitality Affects operate is given by Stern, demonstrating how this capacity functions in adults' spiritual life: "Abstract dance and music are examples par excellence of the expressiveness of Vitality Affects. Dance reveals to the viewer-listener multiple vitality affects and their variations, without resorting to plot or categorical affect signals from which the Vitality Affects can be derived. The choreographer is most often trying to express a way of feeling, not a specific content of feeling. This example is particularly instructive, because the infant, when viewing parental behavior that has no intrinsic expressiveness, may be in the same position as the viewer of abstract dance, or the listener to music. The manner of performance of a parent's act expresses a Vitality Affect, whether or not the act is some categorical affect."

K: I have no idea how Amodal Perception relates to Expressive Arts Therapy. Can you explain this to me?

A: Amodal Perception is the baby's innate capacity to perceive the world in a holistic intermodal sensational form. By way of Amodal Perception, the baby takes information, received in one sensory modality, and somehow translates it into another sensory modality. By using this capacity, the pre-verbal infant transports "a metaphorical-affect" to the other, and Stern labels this metaphorical affect: Vitality affect. *We may, therefore, identify Amodal Perception in Expressive Arts Therapies and Coaching, when a client expresses him/herself in one modality, while simultaneously stimulated and encouraged by others working in other modalities. Their response should include gestures indicating that a Vitality Affect is perceived, namely, the individual will show signs of cooperation with the other modalities, while still involved with his or her activity.* For example: A client is attached to his piece of art and, for therapeutic reasons (see in chapter two: Conditions for Intermodality), he shift into a movement creation axis. In such a moment of spontaneous, intuitive artistic flow, we cannot allow ourselves start lecturing or teaching the performing client what we expect him to do or how to act. It's the same in a group, we cannot talk while dancing or playing. If we talked, we would spoil the creative performance and would ruin the chance to get the fourth sort of meaning, the Secret. The Secret comes out of spontaneity, in a trance-like state, where you allow the artistic language to express itself spontaneously. So how can we possibly communicate with each other while we perform? Only through Amodal Perception. This means that the client, while still with his eyes closed in the middle of the circle, can sense a group member approaching her, not through verbal communication, but she hears the steps and the breathing, both move their hands in circles in the air, she in the horizontal and he in the vertical direction, harmonizing in a fabulous turmoil of four hands. This synchronicity is made through the Amodal Perception ability to sense her movement and attune, duplicating with his own parallel version. This is a fantastic suggestive, hypnotic way of non-verbal communication, This wonderful holistic and sensational capacity, where you can work in harmony by transmitting emotions through the senses, starts at such an early phase in our lives, right after birth, communicating on the same modality, voice to voice, or cross modal, voice attuned to movement.

K: Intuitively, I get the feeling that we should connect here Amodal Perception with trust and depth? I asked how it relates to expressive art, meaning why would you use this concept? This concept, I think, is not just used to explain how you engage in the intermodal, by not speaking or leading the client. Rather, in my opinion, it reverts the client back to childhood, gives him a feeling of proper attunement, and thus establishes trust, which leads to depth, which grants proper psychological conditions for the client to work on his initial "wound." Is that so?

A: You followed me very well. Trust is often built not through verbal negotiations, but rather through intentional sensory interaction, mostly among artists, musicians and actors. The same way that we can correspond with our clients by using the Amodal Perception in a communicative mode, so the client understands through sensual gestures what we suggest, and reacts accordingly.

Here is how you should apply these modes of communication (Attunement and Amodal Perception), when facing an artwork done by your client. You have to attune not only to the client, but also to his artistic production. The artifact, the movement and sound all possess traits, scars, fractions, nuances, and they all own a spirit, just like the human being who created them and engaged in the experience. Actually, the Creation Axis paradigm derives from an empathic approach, in that it traces, in precision, the step-by-step path the client advances along in his creative production.

K: Can you give me an example?

A: I shall bring up an example which starts with a demonstration for the application of Amodal Perception in a group therapy context and ends up with a discussion on True or False Selves.

Imagine a workshop, and Sara wishes to relate to her clay red ball, which she painted in a heavy red gouache glaze. The artwork is still wet, and she naturally holds it in her two hands. My impression is that the ball is stuck in its moist texture to her hands, turning it into a continuous sensitive extension of herself. I urged her to work intermodally, and let the ball lead her into movement. While she stood up, holding the ball in front of her, I asked her to attune to the needs of the ball ("What does this clay ball need?") and, in response, she immediately straightened her hands, allowing her red ball to lead her, as if it were the head of an arrow. At this point, I applied Amodal Perception by playing music: A woman's voice connected to freedom (my own association). The melody and feminine voice harmonized with Sara's dance. This attunement to her ball's needs led her movement into a most beautiful dance, bequeathing sensations of freedom, versatile aerodynamic movements associated with daring, expanding her narrow restricted basic repertoire. When she gathered herself, and ended her small performance, and after she reported about her insights, members of the group shared their impressions of the performed dance. This is the Amodal Perception. Now see how it turned into a True versus False Self issue. At that point, one of the members of the group, out of authentic intuition, allowed himself to step out from the impressed point of view of the audience, empathized with her movement and said to himself aloud: "Wow, I think this is made up." When he sampled it, he wondered, why everybody was impressed, whereas while he sat there, he felt nothing. For him, apparently, it turned out to be a false dance. In the group context, we held a serious discussion where Sara claimed she had enjoyed the dance, but actually her goal had been to break the ball, and discover the meaning of the inner blue space she had hidden inside the ball which, for her, was opposing the red exterior glaze. We were surprised at how powerful her false self dance was. We were all attentive to her need to go on with the artistic Creation Axis and elaborate on breaking the red ball to expose the blue core, and encouraged her, later on, to dialogue with the blue essence which had so attracted her attention.

Heintz Kohut's concepts as applied to clinical expressive arts therapies and coaching

Heinz Kohut was an Austrian American psychoanalyst best known for his development of Self Psychology, an influential school of thought within psychodynamic/psychoanalytic theory which helped transform the modern practice of analytic and dynamic treatment approaches.

K: Winnicott talks about the Good Enough Mother, but this idealistic parental image grants a norm that needs to be fulfilled, otherwise it calls for psychological problems, psychosomatic and otherwise. Is it never fulfilled according to the idealistic desire?

A: Your question is leading us directly to Heintz Kohut's theory about the Self.

Nowadays, most people who refer to clinics report on those parent-child early life experiences, and they are narcissistically wounded. Kohut (1971) sketches the character of the narcissistic client as one who "will describe subtly experienced, yet pervasive feelings of emptiness and depression which, in contrast to the conditions in the psychosis and borderline states, are alleviated as soon as the narcissistic transference has become established - but which become intensified when the relationship to the therapist or coach is disturbed...he is not fully real...his emotions are dulled... he is doing his work without zest...he seeks a routine to carry him along, since he appears to be lacking in initiative." In surveying various categories of the narcissistic client's functioning ego, Kohut describes "in the sexual sphere, perverse fantasies, or lack of interest in sex; in the social sphere work inhibitions, inability to form and maintain significant relationships, delinquent activities; in his manifest personality features we see lack of humor, lack of empathy for other people's needs and feelings, lack of sense of proportion, a tendency towards attacks of uncontrolled rage, pathological lying."

The most severe cases that come to private clinics, as a result of basic breaks in childhood, are borderline personality disorder, narcissistic disorder, depressive or manic depressive disorders, anxiety and obsessive compulsive disorders. These syndromes, starting from narcissistic disorder to borderline personality, are people who suffer from a crack in the development of their Self, the Self as defined by Donald Winnicott (1971), Heinz Kohut (1971), Daniel Stern (1985), Christopher Bollas (1987), Thomas Ogden (1989) and others we have cited. That sense of self grants us high or adequate self-esteem, self-confidence, self-introspection, the ability to stay by ourselves calmly, self-sufficiently and in a state of self-satisfaction.

I shall share with you first my initial experience, whenever I start a process with a client. When we first meet for intake and contract, I realize there are two personalities in the room (relating to my client). My client's Persona, meaning his appearance, the one who steps through my door, sits, complains and wishes to arrive at a change in his or her life. The other personality exists as well, from day one, yet it requires a deeper observation to grasp the inner personality with which I am trying to correspond, to which I am trying to transmit knowledge, insight and emotional empathy, as if my client is a box, and inside the box there is another entity, which is the potential personality which will eventually absorb the chance to create change and turn suffering into a relatively happier or more satisfactory life. This hidden psychic personality is my client's Self.

In relating to Self Psychology, we are dealing with the reconstruction of that Self. The Self is that inner entity of a person which grants him with awareness, potential, self-esteem, courage, wisdom and intuition, hope to overcome obstacles in life. This is the inner friend, to whom I transmit my relatedness in the therapeutic and coaching context.

Kohut (1984) used the concept Cohesive Self, meaning an integrated consolidation of this internal database, granting the belief that I am not alone, I am by my Self and my Self is an actual negotiated, touchable, inner sensation or notion which enables me to be on my own, make my own decisions and connect to my genuine authentic lifestyle.

K: So, the Self would be some inner entity that has the strength to resist social conformed decision?

A: The Self is an adaptive mechanism that, on the one hand, tells you what you are, what you're worth, what your needs are but, at the same time, it helps you to tolerate a situation where you have to conform, join in, assimilate, you do not lose your true Self, but there is a false Self which helps you to manage and bridge towards the external social world. The Self is an awareness of your inner needs and it facilitates your adaptations, according to your environment's expectations, so you may function properly.

K: How is the Self, according to Self Psychology, created?

A: Kohut (1985), in explaining how we develop and integrate a cohesive self, says that for an integrated Self to develop, we must provide for the baby two psychological conditions. One, corresponding to Winnicott's "Mirroring," is "Fascination," meaning giving positive feedback. The Parental Image needs to provide the baby with three psychological needs: morroring, twinship and idealization in order to show the baby that he is acknowledged. But if only this psychic ingredient is applied, the child becomes egocentric, manic and ego-inflated. So, there must be another applied ingredient, which Kohut termed "Optimal Frustration." The infant, being admired and loved, learns to tolerate frustration. While inevitably frustrated, the infant gets a chance to fantasize until he will be finally gratified. In this gap of time between "I am frustrated and I want my milk" to "Here is my milk," there is an Intermediate Phase where the child imagines the milk coming and this builds a preliminary condition for learning processes. Every learning process is a frustrating process, and in order to overcome a frustrating process, one has to believe in the outcome, before the outcome is achieved. This simulation of waiting in ambiguity in an obscure situation is based on Kohut's (1971) principle of Optimal Frustration. Eventually the Optimal Frustration must end with gratification. This is how the Self is built.

Most clients who engage in therapy or coaching come to us because their Self is not integrated. Either they were not admired and respected, or they were too frustrated in previous times in life.

Let's take the "Self point of view," and check to see where it is positioned on the Artistic Psychodynamic Triangle.

I assume that the client comes to therapy

because his Self is not integrated. It's either that he is narcissistically wounded (feels ashamed, easily gets hurt or suffers from rage or anger or jealousy) or has anxiety attacks or is obsessive-compulsive or depressed. This inner friend - the Self - is not functioning well. It's like he hasn't got the gravitational power that holds him together and connects him to his inner truth, to his Self.

The artifact, once personified and allowed to speak (through the I-Thou Gestalt technique), usually represents the True Self of the client. The artifact, when you locate it in contrast to the client, will always represent a cohesive authentic self. I will give you an example from a session that I recently had.

I have a client, Monica, who is in bad shape now: Her husband left her, she suffers from anxiety attacks and cannot be by herself. I dared to ask her, to face her Self with the Gestalt technique of the empty chair. I asked her to tell the empty chair (which was nominated to represent her Self) how terrible she feels, because her husband had left her, and she could not fall asleep anymore. She started to complain to the Self (located on the empty chair). When she finished complaining to the Self (located in the empty chair), I asked her to move to the empty chair and become her own Self. The moment she moved to the chair (Self), her body language totally changed, her voice became calm and the inner voice on the empty chair said to her: "I hear you, how can I help you?" The moment she moved back to become herself, already in my studio, we had a new entity which became her inner helper. Whenever she moved back to the Self position, signified by the empty chair, we experienced a calmed down, relaxing integrated small space in her overwhelmed personality, to which she could connect.

This is the landscape of the Self of which we speak. The art productions can present a benign, healthy, strong, authentic internal power which offers the client a solution, comfort and containment. This is a paradox because, fifteen minutes earlier, a client created a sculpture and, twenty minutes later, this sculpture automatically became a healer, an icon that knows what is best for the client who has just created it.

Let me also relate to the Expressive Therapist in this situation. The Expressive Therapist or Coach needs to give up on his ego, in order to enable the client to discover the healing powers of the Self, which are imbedded in the art. The coach/therapist needs to move from a knowing, consulting, independent figure who operates on the client and knows what is beneficial for the client, locating himself in a position of a *mediator*, one who helps the client address, directly, his needs towards the art object, in order to suck out the knowledge and healing power which the art contains for the client. The therapist needs to actually move away, so that the dialogue will be held between client and art, nevertheless you cannot ignore and simply move away, because you have to connect the client to the artwork by saying mediating words, such as "so the art said" and "so you said" (like a reporter on TV). When the therapist identifies a significant sentence that either is said by the client or is heard from the artwork, the therapist has to intervene, asking the client or artifact to *repeat this sentence three times*, so that the client gets to understand the healing sentence and it's applicative meaning. *The artifact functions, in this case, as an Artistic Self-Object.*

Object Relations Applied to Expressive Arts Therapy & Coaching

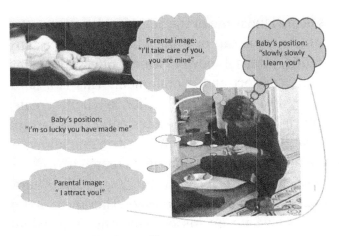

K: What is a "Self-Object?"

A: The theory of Self Psychology claims that the baby is born with a "sense of a self" (Stern, 1985) or a developed self (Kohut, 1984), and describes precise conditions for a cohesive self to develop. Now "Self-Object" is Kohut's (1971) definition of *the baby's imaginative perception of the Parental Image. I need to stress here that the concept of Self-Object is crucial for understanding the whole paradigm of the Psychodynamic Triangle. There is an actual parental figure (Mom, Dad or any significant other), however Kohut explains that the actual interaction of the baby with the significant other creates, in the baby's psyche, in the baby's imagination, a new image, the image of the internalized care giver, and this image is concieved by the baby as "Me-Not Me" image which developes into the Self-Object: A new hero on the baby's internal imaginative psychic theatrical stage. This Me-Not Me is in the essence of the dialoigue between our c;lient (in Expressive Arts Therapy & Coaching) and the artifact.*

In Kohut's words, he relates to "a developmental

phase in which the child attempts to save the original narcissism by giving it over to a narcissistically experienced omnipotent and perfect Self-Object."

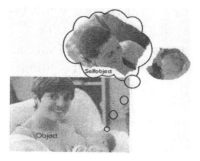

The child perceives the parent image as a Self-Object, in order to create a cohesive Self. "Under favorable circumstances, the child gradually faces the realistic limitations of the idealized Self object, gives up the idealizations, makes transmuting re-internalizations" and internalizes the sense of the Self-Object. (This corresponds to Melanie Klein's approach, describing the internal fantastic process the baby experiences in his inner imagination, in the presence of the realistic maternal figure). As Kohut (1984) puts it, later on: "The 'You' plays a great role in supporting the cohesion, strength, and harmony of the Self, that is, to the experience of the 'You' (maternal figure) as Self-Object." "You" is the target of the baby's desire and love and the target of his anger and aggression. Kohut knew that this dyad of the "Self-Self-Object" relationship forms the essence of psychological life, from birth to death.

Kohut (1985) later on considers the issue of *Self-Object surrogates* ,and he (the infant) used to simultaneously touch certain soft Self-Object surrogates (the silky rim of a blanket) and stroke his own skin (the lobe of the ear) and hair, thus creating a psychological situation of merger with a non-human Self-Object that he totally controls, and thereby depriving himself of the opportunity to experience the structure-building optimal failures of a human Self-Object."

This quotation relating to a surrogate Self-Object is crucial to our discussion, as it validates my approach, claiming that *a personified artifact may function for the client as an artistic Self-Object.*

K: I think you're starting to explain to me about the Artistic Self-Object. Are you?

A: Indeed. I have an image in my head. If this image is expressed by art, it means I went through the Creation Axis and "gave birth" to an artistic product. I assume that this image I have made, being personified, can speak out loud, uttering not only what my consciousness can speak through it, but even that I could speak my authentic intentions, reveal unconscious materials, testify my real truth, present my good enough Parental Image, cure myself by possessing my hidden genuine knowledge, feelings and somatic sensations then, all in a whole, it functions as an *Artistic Self-Object* for me.

Let me return finally now to that six-year-old girl who ended up finally in therapy with me, the girl who lost her father before she had known him, and let us return to her hair. Hair, in symbolism, is designating femininity on the one hand, but also power, as demonstrated in the Biblical story, in the case of Samson. In one of our sessions, she mentioned to me: "Did Mom tell you that my father left me when I was a baby?" Sitting near her, as a masculine therapeutic figure, I simply admired that little girl's strength to bring up her loss in my presence. I suggested we searched for her father in the magazines, and put in front of her a big pile of journals, scissors, glue and white paper, with the intention to collect pictures of father images she will associate with. It was amazing how this girl created an Artistic Self-Object, in search of men engaged in specific activities and roles, emerging randomly from the magazines to finally assemble the overall profile of her desired, imagined Dad.

The easiest way to explain what the Artistic Self-Object represents is to imagine a mother nursing a baby. We can diminish this interaction between the mother and the baby suckling her breast solely to the feeding level. But there is an extra, terribly important psychological phenomena, held in between provider and the consumer. The maternal figure expresses love, because the moment the baby suckles at her breast, she feels relief and even slight pleasure seeing her own child functioning well, vigorous and efficient. She is full of contentment. This baby seems an extension of herself, as just recently he was integral part of her body. Yet now it's time to inquire as to what happens in the baby's mind. If the baby is very vigorous and gluttonous, he may fantasize about himself swallowing his mother's breast, the pleasure may turn into sadistic cannibalism (as Melanie Klein suggests). The maternal image gradually consolidates in the baby's imagination and creates an inner presentation of the maternal figure, an inner fantasy of the paternal image, either positive or negative (parallel to Klein's good and bad breast, of which we spoke previously). If the parent-image provides the baby with optimal psychological conditions (admiration and limited frustration), a cohesive nuclear Self can emerge. Self-Object is fantasy and a lifetime necessity. I find Ra'anan Kulka (1991), a famous Israeli Self psychologist, to have a definition of Self-Object that is very interesting. He says: "What, in fact, is the psychic situation of being a Self-Object? To turn into a Self-Object for the other, you agree to give your Self 'up' for the sake of the Selfhood" of another that is embodied in you - to be, for him, a Self outside of himself, so that he may observe his Selfhood in you, recognize himself in you, internalize his Self through you. He thus becomes a unique self, not by a process of identification in the accepted sense of the term. The experiential significance of this situation, for the analyst, is one of great loneliness, at times a complete abrogation of sources of narcissistic satisfaction, a virtual giving up of one's own psychic place - a kind of acceptance of "being erased," which is not identical to being nothing, or to nothingness. On the contrary, this is a situation that demands a most intensive psychic presence, having complex characteristics of passive activity and the dissolution of boundaries between Self and other, without breaking a single boundary."

In Expressive Therapies and Coaching, we may identify the Self-Object when clients treat their artistic product as their newborn creature, and naturally take over the role of Self object to the personified artistic production. At first, clients perceive their artistic work as unfamiliar and incomprehensible, but the more preoccupied with it they become, the more this work stimulates them, and functions as a Self-Object for them. In addition, the therapist observes the client's artistic self, shows curiosity, interest and involvement, thereby allowing the artistic product to function for him/her as Self-Object.

K: This is so deep. Now what is Empathy according to Kohut, and how is it compared to Stern's Affect Attunement?

A: *Affect Attunement* is a spontaneous reaction of the maternal figure, and it leans on the instincts. Kohut's *Empathic Attunement* is a basic concept in Kohut's Self psychology. Let's differentiate between attunement and empathic Attunement, because these are very basic practical techniques in Expressive Arts Therapies.

Attunement is spontaneous, instinctive, sensational resonance with the other. Empathic Attunement, however, is a learned way of communication, it's artificial. Empathy is the capacity to think and feel oneself into the inner life of another. It is our ability to experience, to an extent, what another person is experiencing. Empathy is the nature of the early mother-child relationship.

In therapy, it is a fundamental and essential observational technique which the therapist must possess, in order to obtain psychological data about the patient. It is a basic component in helping the patient restore his disintegrated self, and it is achieved by the therapist's efforts to move out from himself with warmth, and sympathize with the patient's attitude, position or feeling. When you sample the inner space of the other, in a holistic way, you can sort out what the person possibly is thinking, feeling and sensing. If he is fearful, enthusiastic, enraged, I want to be able to savor his fear, enthusiasm or rage. Kohut (1985) says that, inevitably, we cannot possibly be empathic constantly. Even towards ourselves. He coined the concept of *Empathic Failure*. He said that empathic failure is also curative, because it causes optimal frustration. In his words: "The child's experiences during the oedipal phase become understandable only when they are considered within the matrix of the empathic, partially empathic, or un-empathic responses from the side of the Self object aspects of his environment." Kohut maintains that "the optimal parent is not the genius whose Self is absorbed by his creative activities and whose Self extensions relate only to his work, and to those people who can be experienced by him as aspects of his work. Optimal parents - again I should rather say optimally failing parents, are people who, despite their stimulation by, and competition with the rising generation, are also sufficiently transient participants in the ongoing stream of life, so as to be able to experience the growth of the next generation with unforced, non-defensive joy." In his third book, Kohut (1984) includes a concise summary of the stages of the development of the cohesive self: "First, a basic intuneness must exist between the Self and its Self-Objects. Second, Self-Object failures (e.g., responses based on faulty empathy) of a non-traumatic degree must occur. We refer to the results of such failures on the part of the Self-Objects of childhood as "optimal frustrations."

K: How is Empathy connected to Expressive Arts Therapies?

A: *In Expressive Arts Therapies, you can identify the coach or therapist's empathic approach, when they are seen locating themselves near the ego boundaries of the client: Their position and body posture are reminiscent of a parental image, observing, guarding, and assisting the client. Or they may be seen imitating or following the client's artistic gestures, in order to further understand the meaning or intention of their client. Sometimes, the coach or therapist may join in the client's experience with closed eyes, in order to eliminate external interruptions and increase his attunement to the client's rhythm, movement, lines...or they may convey their understanding and participation with the client by his harmonic use of sound, gesture and color. Finally, they may try to reconstruct, follow the stages and learn the technique and chronology of the artistic product from the client. By this they can achieve real understanding of the process which their client has gone through.*

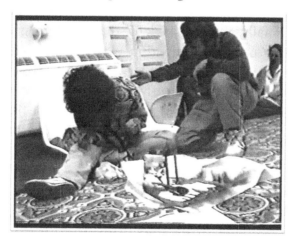

I intuitively developed the Creation Axis paradigm, because I had a feeling that the expressive therapist needed to have a diagnostic responsibility to be able to systematically trace the steps of the process of creativity, not from a projective external judgmental attitude (which is diminishing and imposes a clinical point of view on the client), but rather from the inside of the experience, understanding the psychodynamic factors of the Contact with artistic media, to be empathic to the Contact, imagine the fingers of the client when he's hesitant to open the cellophane and take Plasticine out. See the feeling and the sensation of clumsiness when he takes a plastic glass of water and it is splashed on the rug on the way to his artwork, when he tries to organize himself, shifting from excitement to clumsiness, trying to create something he maybe has already had in mind. Then empathize with the feeling, the sensational and intellectual levels of how he starts to improvise, the fear of the unknown, the fear of mistakes, the creative hints of the original prototypes, the way that the components are compounded together. Avoid a teacher's approach and rather experience the creative process from up close. Finally, when asked by the client to give him feedback, use this empathic experience to nurture the client with feedback that will be appropriate to this capacity to absorb. By adopting this approach, you become an assuring and a trustworthy figure to the client. For me, this is empathy in Expressive Arts Therapies and Coaching.

K: So, it's the therapist's role to empathically connect with the client's artwork, to help him understand the client's dilemma, to lead him through a process where he can relate to the art from zero distance with the I-Thou Gestalt technique?

A: Yes, however this is not the only role for the therapist. While the client is moving in the space, or playing an instrument, or singing, or creating a piece of art, and you - the therapist - express yourself near the client (while he is moving, or singing or presenting his artwork) by locating yourself connected to the ego boundaries of the client and his artwork, you create a *triangular framework* (the therapist, the client and his artwork). This triangle is a psychodynamic space made out of emotions, ideas and physical needs, all combined into an expressive performance. Let me stress that the difference between common coaching or therapy (where the change is hopefully caused in the intimate space between the two) in the Expressive Arts Therapies the "*psychodynamic triangle*" is the healing factor which will onset change.

Let me explain the meaning of this photo, which clarifies the therapeutic potential of each of the three poles of the "psychodynamic triangle:"

Pole 1 - The client is in the role of a parent and the artwork is in baby's role. From this pole, she may say to the baby: "I will take care of you, you are mine." Still, from this same pole, she may say, as a criticizing mother: "I made you and you're very ugly and I'm so disappointed." By this, she identifies with the castrating mother.

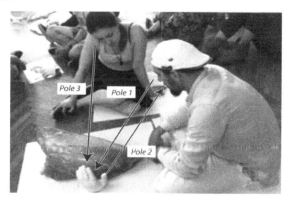

Pole 2 - If we change roles, and now the baby as art can start talking as a parent, it can say "I attract you." The baby (as a parent now) may also say: "I know you made efforts to make me beautiful, I respect your intention, as I was born out of your inspiration." So, we have a "parental child," who empowers the creator, as a good enough mother.

Pole 3 - The other side of the triangle is when the therapist makes contact with the personified artistic product of the client and talks to it.

I shall share with you a vignette: A client named Mike talks to the dance he recently performed. I ask the client "what is the meaning of the dance for you?" He responds, "I expressed my freedom." Now he can talk to "Freedom." What was this movement you just experienced? He says "suppression." He can talk to "Suppression." *You have to turn the movement or the music into a metaphor.* The movement and music are more difficult to dialogue with than plastic art, which is tangible. Movement and music, once stopped, no longer have their physical presence, and they remain only on the kinesthetic or audio memory levels. *In order to hook them, you must code them by way of metaphor.* This is why musical pieces are labeled with metaphorical names: Beethoven's Moonlight or Stravinsky's the Rite of Spring, or Vivaldi's Four Seasons.

Mike says to Freedom: "It's so hard to reach you, usually I dwell naturally on your other side the 'suppression'" (Pole 1). If he moves to sit in front of himself and takes the place of the metaphor, Freedom, and talks to himself (the dancer), he takes over the role of a mother to her baby, from the movement point of view. "Freedom/dance" may say: "Yes, it is indeed quite hard to achieve me, but see how finally you overcame suppression and gained me."

I, as therapist – Pole 3 – may intervene and talk to Mike's Freedom: "Now that he gained you, what needs to be done to keep you?" The metaphor "Freedom/dance" (through Mike) may answer: "Just be aware of my existence, keep in touch." In further retrospective discussion, we can arrive at insights about what will help Mike keep this valuable awareness of his need for existing Freedom and, on a practical level, what he can do.

K: Why is this important to "name" this movement or music?

A: I'll answer through another example. If the client (Rona) holds a piece of made art, she is situated in the Parental Image (the mother) role, and the art is her baby. But if Rona enables her artifact talk, through the autonomy of the image principle, to her - then Rona becomes the baby and the artifact, the dance or musical metaphor turn into a parental image (mother) for Rona. This is an immense therapeutic opportunity which opened up through the paradoxical dialogue.

K: It only becomes a paradox when the artifact took on the role of mothering its own creator, but if you look at it from a time unit point of view, first you "mother" the artistic product, and then it changes roles, because the baby becomes the mother to you. Then it is indeed a healing process.

A: Bravo, fantastic.

K: But what about the coach or the therapist? You mentioned that they are involved in the triangle and actually make up the third pole?

A: This is the third pole in the triangle, and this pole is targeted at the therapist's counter-transference towards his client, but even more towards his or her artistic product. Remember, we encouraged the therapist to step into the client's ego boundaries and attune to his artwork. When this happens, the therapist is affected, (may be sometimes infected) by the artistic dramatic, aesthetic, dynamic artifact. The client's created Main Theme might have evoked the therapist memories, emotions, anxieties and traumas. Often do we see Expressive Therapists crying in the presence of their client's artistic acts. If the therapist connects to the artistic outcome, tries the movement, joins the melody or dialogues, not only does he empathize, not only is he attuned, but he also may discover that his client's metaphor functions as a good enough mother to him, or as a threatening parental image. Such an experience will be of help for the therapist or coach to relate to the client from a more objective approach, as his awareness has increased. He doesn't act blindly in the dramatic situation. If the therapist faced difficulty during the encounter with the artistic production, it surely calls for supervision.

K: How can we claim that the created artwork is the Self-Object of the client? How can we claim that what the client makes presents his Self-Object, and not just an imaginative, arbitrary instance?

A: When Winnicott spoke about the "Transitional Object" (Objects of affection which the child soothes itself and function as substitute for the mother), he layed down the idea of playing as crucial for internalizing the Parental Image. This playfulness creativity onsets the "Me-Not Me" game. Here is where the dialogue with the artifact in Expressive Therapy & Coaching comes into the picture.

The developmental process Kohut described for the Self-Object and its psychological importance to the infant is identical to the process described for a client who creates an artifact. If I made an artwork, I will end up with an image. From now on, I am not interested in the realistic object which I made or performed. I am interested in the image which I keep and will remain in my head (my visual, kinesthetic or audio sensation).

Self-Object (surrogate Self-Object or Artistic Self-Object) is an introjected internal image (either with positive or negative connotations), which has been gradually crystallized through interaction with the real significant figure that exists in reality. The dialogue with the artifact which we actually made fits totally with the internalization of the maternal figure.

Let's analyze the following process: When we witness a client creating or performing, we should assume that, prior to the onset of the Creation Axis, he has already had an idea in his mind (at least an inspiration). Meaning that, before you started the Creation Axis, an unknown idea and motivation was present, which Christopher Bollas (1992) called *Genera*. This vague thought starts to crystallize and actualize itself through the Creation Axis. When the client arrives at the fourth stage, the Main Theme, we can see a reflection of the idea that was on the client's mind, before he stepped into the Creation Axis. This genetic artistic birth turns into an image. If the client personifies that image, we are permitted to relate to it as an Artistic Self-Object.

K: Before we arrive at the Main Theme in the Creation Axis, there is the "How" stage. Can the "How" stage also give us hints about the quality of the coming Artistic Self-Object?

A: How the client approaches the assignment of bringing to life his creative idea can give hints about his attitude towards the artistic outcome. If the artistic outcome complies with the artist's expectation, we may witness, later in their dialogue, a positive, supportive, empathic Artistic Self-Object. However, if the Creation Axis is typical of restlessness and negative comments towards the created art, then we may have two options for the Artistic Self-Object: It may either be compassionate and comforting (trying to heal its creator like a "parental child"), or we shall witness a vengeance object.

K: You mentioned that there is another side of the psychodynamic triangle, the therapist and the artwork communicational connection. Can you explain more about it to me?

A: Okay, let's look at the therapist in this drama. The artistic object, once starting to speak to the client, inevitably affects also the therapist. For example, if the movement that the client called "Freedom" calls for the client's freedom, and the therapist is mothering the client into a "freedom quest," maybe the therapist will face one of two "wounded healer" experiences. If the therapist suffers also from suppression, he inevitably will identify, through counter-transference, with this metaphoric artistic speech about freedom. The therapist may perform modeling, experiencing himself in dialogue with the metaphor (freedom). This is how he can help the client arrive at better insights about this issue. Example: Says the therapist, "I will speak now to the movement of freedom, so that you (the client) hear how much I praise and reinforce it for you (the client) to adopt this approach."

The second option is for the therapist, through counter-transference with the artistic product, to hold a supervisory dialogue and discuss the meaning of the Artistic Self-Object for himself. This act also strengthens the client, as he witnesses his therapist courageously dealing with an artifact made by him. This is so empathic, in a Kohutian approach.

K: What does it mean, "self supervision?"

A: It means that I am dealing with this dilemma you brought up through your artifact for my own sake, but also to improve my role as your therapist.

K: Is this the only connection to the therapist in the triangle?

A: Yes, for your own sake and for the client's sake.

K: So, in one instance you're connecting to the artistic product, because it draws your attention, because of your longing for freedom, but you're connecting to the client, because your communication with the freedom is empowering the client, and this is the other line of the triangle.

A: I would like to distance a moment and sum up the issue in a comprehensive way. Whenever expressing ourselves through the senses, the performed art is inspired by an imaginative inner source. External stimulants like music, space and materials effect our imagination. This stimulating external mechanism is well-known as "projection." We project our inner world onto available objects. We actually can distinguish, through the Creation Axis, how an idea gradually crystallizes in reality and turns into a Main Theme (art product, dance, or melody). Something in our psychic internal world is being created through the arts. We must not forget that when we look at the dance of a dancer, listen to a melody played by musician, or look at a readymade sculpture, in the performer's psyche there has been formatted an image presentation of the invented art. Are they the same? No, this discrepancy (between the actualized art which we witness and the internal image of the art which was its inspiration) is an important psychodynamic issue. This is what is causing despair or dissatisfaction, when the real artistic object doesn't correspond to the internal image. The source of the internal image can be rooted in the maternal figure in childhood, or from previous significant events in life. The imaginative and the actual are embedded in mother-child relationships. Once we let the external image talk, it functions as an "ambassador" of the internal image, and this fits the phenomena of the Artistic Self-Object. Kohut says that the maternal figure gradually is internalized and becomes intrapsychic. The maternal figure, or this artistic idea, held in intrapsychic perception, while practically actualized, becomes true, can be admired, yet also can be experienced as limited and frustrating, as it will establish inwards an Artistic Self-Object. It's a fantasy. We always need such an internal Self-Object to accompany our life experiences. As Kohut speaks about a surrogate or substitute Self-Object, we can assume the artwork may stand for the substitute Artistic Self-Object.

Paradoxically, the same artistic Self-Object – client relationships exist for the coach or therapist who witnesses this process. They, too, are obliged to endure a silent or overt dialogue with the client's Artistic Self-Object.

References

Bick, E. (1968) "The Experience of the Skin in Early Object Relations." In: International Journal Psychoanalysis. 1968;49(2):484-6.

Biran, H. (2015) The Courage of Simplicity: Essential Ideas in the Work of W.R. Bion. Karnac Books.

Bollas, C. (1987). The Shadow of The Object, Free Association Books, London.

Bollas, C. (1991). Forces of Destiny, Free Association Books, London.

Bollas, C. (1992). Being A Character, Routledge, London.

Davis, M. & Wallbridge, D. (1981) Boundary and Space, An Introduction to the Work of D.W. Winnicott, Penguin Books.

Hinshelwood, H.D (1991) A Dictionary of Kleinian Thought, Free Association Book, London.

Klein, M. (1929) "Infantile Anxiety Situations Reflected in a Work of Art." International Journal Psycho - Anal., Vol 10.

Klein, M. (1932), The Psychoanalysis of Children. Hogarth, London.

Klein, M. (1946), "Notes on Some Schizoid Mechanisms" in: Developments in Psycho-Analysis, London: Hogarth Press (1952) 292-320.

Kohut, H. (1971). The Analysis of the Self, International Universities Press, Inc. Madison-Connecticut.

Kohut, H. (1977). The Restoration of the Self, Int. U. Press.

Kohut, H. (1978). Creativeness, Charisma, Group Psychology. The Search for the Self, (ed.) Orenstein, New York Int. U. Press, 2, 793-843.

Kohut, H. (1984). How Does Analysis Cure? The University of Chicago Press.

Kohut, H. (1985). Self Psychology and the Humanities, Norton and com. New York.

Kulka, R. (1991). Reflections on the Future Development of Self Psychology. The Evolution of Self Psychology, Ed. Goldberg A. The Analytic Press, Hillsdale, N.J. 7, 175.

Mahler, M. (1975). The Psychological Birth of the Human Infant, Maresfield Library, London.

Miller, A. (1979), Das Drama des Begabten Kindes, und die Suche nach wahren Selbst. Surkamp Verlag. Hebrew rights by Dvir Pub. House, Tel Aviv, 1992.

Mitchel, M. (1991) The Selected Melanie Klein, Penguin Books, Middlesex, England.

Ogden, T. (1989) The Primitive Edge of Experience. Hebrew translation: Am Oved Pub. Ltd Tel Aviv 2001

Stern, D. (1985). The Interpersonal World of the Infant, Basic Books.

Winnicott, D. (1960). "Ego Destruction in Terms of True and False Self." In Winnicott, The Maturational Processes and the Facilitating Environment, pp 140-152. In: Bacal, H.A & Newman, K.M (1990) Theories of Object Relations: Bridges to Self Psychology, Columbia University Press, New York.

Winnicott, D. (1966). "The Ordinary Devoted Mother. Talk given to the Nursing School Association of Great Britain and Northern Ireland, London Branch." In: Bacal, H. A. & Newman, K. M. (1990) Theories of Object Relations: Bridges to Self Psychology, Columbia University Press, New York.

Chapter 6

Diagnostic Thinking in Expressive Arts Therapy & Coaching

Diagnostic Thinking in Expressive Arts Therapy and Coaching

A: As mentioned before, the artistic expressions act upon us with direct immediacy, and spark an experience within us that has a certain extent of projection. Out of empathic responsibility and desire to experience the message objectively, the therapist or coach is in need of a diagnostic point of view.

This gate may cause some readers certain uneasiness. I recall that most my professional life I was labeled by my clinical psychology colleagues as "too expressive," and by my Expressive Arts Therapy peers as "too clinical." These attributions were made because I insisted on hanging onto a diagnostic point of view while analyzing my clients' artworks, where elsewhere, while at work, I would go as expressive as possible, for the client's sake. Nevertheless, let's differentiate, right at the beginning here, between *diagnostic thought* to *diagnostic conclusion*.

• *Diagnostic thought* is dynamic, opening up assumptions, enabling the raising of associations, it stimulates and receives possibilities and affiliations. It is the creative aspect, the instinctive and unpredictable part of thought.

• *Diagnostic conclusion* is reductive, logical and binding. Its principal purpose is to enable structuring a clear strategic therapeutic line. Art therapy has a more qualified approach than diagnostic conclusions, which have a tradition of categorizing and placing labels on the client. These conclusions are, by nature, pessimistic and can be a determiner of their fate.

Diagnostic Thinking in Expressive Arts Therapy and Coaching

In this chapter we shall drift from diagnostic thinking to the shores of diagnostic conclusions. While on the shore of diagnostic conclusion, I shall always use the word "may," to assure that we still stay with the assumption and avoid labeling and a judgmental attitude. I shall be doing my best, in this gate, to clarify my diagnostic way of thinking. Often at my seminars and workshop I am asked: "But how did you know? How did you decide to do what you did? Where did you get this idea from?" To answer those questions and more, this chapter presents the keys to my diagnostic intuition.

K: What is the starting point, the source of your diagnostic thinking?

A: Initial diagnostic thought examines the gap between three elements. First, I always look at the *available potential* of the client. The overt, here and now available excellence of the client. This usually emerges and becomes manifest in the first session. Notice what the potential is, the initial talent which you can observe in your client's performance.

Let's take an example and demonstrate how the three dimensions manifest themselves. Daniel, who is fifteen, is referred by the junior high school consultant, because he fails his exams, he is often absent at school, and he has a very bad relationship with some teachers. When we first met, he grabbed papers and markers and I realized Daniel has a "good hand," meaning that he scribbles beautifully. When I express my impression, he says: "Yes, when I was young I used to scribble a lot." So, his available potential to use art is fine.

The second element is the *Norm*. The therapist

compares the initial talent with the norm. What is expected from a person of this age, culture, gender, state of health, etc. In Daniel's case, although the scribbling is beautiful, it appears repeatedly, it fits with someone aged ten and is shrunk. It is expected from adolescents with such talent to express content that fits their age. At age fifteen, they usually use icons, manifest technical objects, show personal style, use achromatic hues, may be even use English words (even if they are not anglophone natives), being fond of the Internet and its language.

Then, I check the data regarding the third element – the *Latent Potential*. What quality can the therapist discover in the latent, hidden potential? What can the coach help the client to further develop? It's the hope, the horizon the therapist holds for the client to reach for. With Daniel, I leaned on his artistic potential and gradually we put aside the markers and planned an artistic project made out of cigarettes (as he was smoking and agreed to collect the packages as raw material with which to improvise).

In movement and music therapy (the ratio between overt, norm and latent potential talents), the diagnostic procedure is the same as in theatrical auditions: The client moves about in the open space, the therapist observes and notices how he is moving (overt) and heeds that he has beautiful movements and very good rhythm. But the therapist may also realize that his knees are weak and tremble, and this is not expected from a young man (norm), this denotes a symbolic meaning or an objective disability, so the therapist may think: "Wow, we should strengthen and develop his muscles (expected norm)." The therapeutic approach, therefore, is based on profiting from her future potential, and the therapist may infer: "Let's see what your knees wish to tell you, dance with them and think how they connect to your maneuvers in life" (latent potential).

It's also very important to remember that diagnostic thought, in the different arts therapies, is based on the combination of three principles: *Experience, organization and content.*

The Expressive therapists or coaches who want to develop their diagnostic skills have to ask themselves three questions in the presence of the client's expressive work.

The *first* one is to ask yourself "What do I experience in the presence of this performance?" Gregg Furth, in his 1988 book *The Secret World of Drawing, Healing through Art* writes: "A picture or drawing always communicates a feeling. It is important to capture the initial, spontaneous impression first and, if possible, to encapsulate it in one word – such as "happy," "sad," "frustrated," "fearful," "confused," rather than evaluating the picture concretely." The importance of "breathing in" subjectively the effect of the artistic product has to do with empathic resonance (previously discussed in Chapter 5).

In movement therapy, while observing a client in an act, you may witness such an experience: The client is moving and you feel that at any moment she might fall, and it is stressful for you, as a viewer. Or, she is dancing so beautifully you want to hug her, it evokes in you compassion. Or, she is so aggressive that you want to stop her. We are in counter-transference domain. We are expected to ask ourselves what feeling the movement, music or art is producing in us. This is one source of data. The level of the therapist's subjective experience in the presence of the artwork.

The *second* is the principle of Organization. There are two levels here to observe: *How* the client manages to express himself in the selected media, and *how* the artwork is organized as a whole and its parts. Here we shall consider factors such as dimensions, composition, rhythms, directions and more. Soon I shall present to you those dimensions systematically and add examples.

The *third* principle is Content. The therapist asks himself, what is the story that this dance or music or art conveys? In the content category, we shall witness the client's desires, conflicts, drives, culture, habits, values, perversions and life story.

K: I must ask you how you prevent yourself from prejudices and a judgmental approach? How can you be sure that what you sample is indeed the truth and applies to the client?

A: I am grateful that you stepped up at this very point. First, let me remind you again and again, it is all about dialoguing with the client. I never impose my observations on my clients, but rather open up options for discussion. Paradoxically, by sharing my observations with the clients, I get more involvement and collaboration from them at the Elaboration phase of the Creation Axis.

Let me explain to you *the rule of "70%,"* which I have developed over the years. You can only be sure enough to make a judgment about your client's work or about the group's acts or behaviors if you can measure *70% of the existing data in a certain artistic reality* or situation. You can only say that this drawing is yellow if it contains more than 70% yellow hues. You can refer to a movement as "staccato" if it is characterized by at least 70% repetitive movements which display short cuts, abrupt gestures and fast kinesthetic changes in a limited sequence of time. You can evaluate a melody as "meditative" if 70% of its length is typically characterized by very slow rhythm and repetitive continuous melody. I sample the rule of 70% to assure my impression is not biased.

K: When you explained to me those three criteria for observation, I felt you changed your intonation and became categorically strict, is that so?

A: Indeed. Finally, our diagnostic tool is our biased personality. Expressive Therapy brings about dramatic performances which affect us emotionally and cognitively. They even shake our psychosomatic responses. How can we diminish our subjectivity and act and respond as objectively as possible, if not through professional standards?

For this, I located those three points of view. When I integrate all of those three data sources, I gain a relatively better understanding of my client's artistic production. One asks what I feel. Two asks how it is organized, and three asks what does it tell me.

K: I'm very interested to learn how to diagnose the chronology, the sequence in which the artistic expression is produced – the Organizational principle. Is this connected with the Organization phase of the Creation Axis?

A: The Organizational phase in the Creation Axis is

partially included in the Organizational Principle. Stages One, Two and Three in the Creation Axis orient us in the client's organizational logistics and style. This is about the "How" issues: How the client is organizing himself, the artistic environment and the artifacts. Remember, we are discussing how the client is organized. In order to understand how the client is organizing his artwork, it is necessary to study its *dimensions*. I start by looking at the *proportion* between the *dimension of the art* and *the artistic quality*.

Dimension of the art and the Artistic Quality

K: What is dimension and what is artistic quality?

A: *Dimension* relates to the aspects of the size of the artifact. In movement, it relates to the space taken, used and explored by the dancer, and in music it relates to the combination of scale, range, frequency and volume the music projects onto the listener. We can simplify this definition by saying that Dimension relates literally to how "big" or "small" the piece of art is. There is a psychodynamic difference between an artistic product which is two-dimensional (like a drawing, a dance held down on the ground while crawling or a monotonous melody) and one presented three-dimensionally. If the art is erected up above, if it corresponds with the space and penetrates the air far above its basis, if the movement performed expands above the ground and the body explores the space, if the melody drifts away from the unison basis of the scale – we shall give a "three-dimensional" attribution to the artifact. If the client is dancing in one place and doesn't move, hardly moving the hands, its effect will be perceived as a small movement. If he expands and dances all over the space, the dimension will be considered big. When it is three-dimensionally oriented, we can assume that the artist wishes to state something "out loud," to emerge into the world with a declaration. This may denote high self-esteem, self-permission to exist and raise up your voice, to declare "here I am" or "Here is my affirmation." Sometimes such artistic production hints upon compensatory needs or grandiosity. The same counts for the opposite. If the work is diminished, tiny, retroflexed, pail and directed inwards, it may leave the impression that the art or the artist is modest, hesitant, careful or inhibited. And again, such withdrawal may hint upon a possible narcissistic wound.

The *Artistic Quality* can be measured by whether or not the art has created a certain tension or emotional impact on the observer. Does it have an impact on your internal experience? If it does, the artistic quality is considered effective, otherwise the quality is doubtful.

At times you may witness that the dimension of the artifact is impressively large, but its artistic impact or quality is very dull. This means that a lot of investment has been given to the outlook on account of cognitive or emotional involvement. The client uses a lot of materials which turn out to be an insignificant mess. We may consider such art as a "manic defense," meaning that the client invests in the surface, in order to consciously or unconsciously hide a wound, a doubt or suffering. Or, the client devotes his experience to sensitive pleasure on account of an intrusive analysis. Sometimes the artwork is very small, but the artistic quality is very effective. This displays a high level of intelligence and sophistication, because much impact is expressed in a very economic manner.

K: I noticed you sometimes say artistic quality and sometimes *artistic message*. Is this the same thing?

A: There is, in my opinion, a direct correlation between the artistic quality and artistic message. Any artifact transmits a psychological message. Even chaotic art transmits a message. When we relate to such artifacts in a context of coaching or therapy, we must be careful not to remain solely on the first impression stanza, but rather to ask ourselves how this artistic expression corresponds to the client's cause of referral.

    It's important to notice if the artistic expression transmits a message to the client. Does it have a meaning for him or her? If the client makes an artistic product and it doesn't have a specific meaning for him, it remains un- useful, from a therapeutic point of view. Unfortunately, many of my colleagues will claim the artistic production in itself is curing, ventilating and grants catharsis. Here is where I prefer to stress my "clinical" approach and connect the coaching and therapeutic quest into the "Secret" concept. In case my clients show a need for catharsis or ventilation for "just having fun," my approach will lead me to question myself, to ask what this activity serves for my client, and what its meaning is considering his or her life these days. Bad artistic quality very often corresponds to poor organization. In any kind of artistic production, you want to discover a certain significance. Then you will find out that, despite poor artistic quality, there is a hidden intention.

K: When you talk about the dimension of the art, you state that you look to see if it's big or small. You observe how much space it takes up. I am not sure what this tells me. Can you further elaborate on this?

A: Along the Creation Axis, between the stages of Contact, Organization and Improvisation, the client may not present a definite Main Theme, but surely the client has a pretense, an expectation for himself, as to what kind of artistic production he wants to present. An aim by which he knows what kind of art he wants to express. It's actually very simple. Maybe you just need an analogy to comprehend it better. If there is a lot of soup in a pot and you want to eat soup, you have to choose a bowl. You may choose a small bowl or a big bowl. The choice of the dimension of the bowl shows how much soup you intend to eat and what you attribute to the container in correlation to its substance.

When a client goes to the art buffet and collects art material or explores the space to start moving or chooses a musical instrument, in the unconscious he already has an intention, an idea or direction of what to do. From that initial point, he starts creating the "bowl" into which he will "pour" the performed art.

I do look at the dimension, but I compare it to the final message. If there is a lot of noise, art material, hectic movement, but nothing comes out, it remains merely a cacophony, debris. It's completely different if we encounter a very "noisy" piece which transmits a strong, harmonious message – a symphony may come out of it. So, I look at the difference between the dimensions and the quality. The proportions between quantity versus quality grant a psycho-diagnostic hypothesis.

K: I can imagine four different outcomes. One is that the *dimension is big and the artistic quality is* "good." Second is when the *dimension is small and the artistic quality is "good."* Third is when the *art is big and artistic quality is "poor,"* and the fourth is when the *dimension is small and the quality is "poor."* Can you explain to me what each means diagnostically?

	+ Dimension -	
+ **Quality**	Big dimension / Good artistic quality	Small dimension / Good artistic quality
-	Big dimension / Bad artistic quality	Small dimension / Bad artistic quality

A: *Big dimension and good artistic quality* shows that the person is talented expressively and he knows how to express himself powerfully through the artistic media, which serves the transmission of the message very well. This is the repertoire of the neurotic who comes for therapy or coaching. It also means that the person can be very dramatic and counts on impressing the observer or himself. As therapists and coaches, we are pleased to work with such artistic productions.

When the client's artistic production falls in the category of *small dimension and impressive artistic quality*, the artistic statement displays either high intelligence and sophistication, or high intelligence and low self-esteem or an inhibited personality. The client is using a minor amount of materials, movement or musical scale, yet succeeds in transmitting or expressing a strong impression of himself onto those who witness his expressive activity. It can also point at modesty, inhibition, defensiveness and obsessive-compulsion, because the client minimizes the artistic outcome and scales it down. An example of such art is the art of Giacometti,

obliging the observer to pay extra attention and maintain attunement. In movement, it would be shown in very tight, small movements characterized by stillness. In music, it will be displayed through a narrow modus (scale), yet with a very effective impact.

Unlike the previous artist, who is using a lot of material to present a strong artistic message, this client succeeds in making a great impact with a lot less material. This means that our second artist is cleverer, more intelligent, more economical, more sophisticated. He is characterized by control and defense, yet expressively is very wise.

K: How does this diagnostic information serve the therapist? Does it give him feedback that he is dealing with a highly intelligent person with a need for control?

A: "Highly intelligent person with a need for control" is only one potential option. You are falling into the trap of over-simplifying the human psyche. *You must always remember that one phenomenon has always more than one explanation.* We tend to over-simplify and arrive at fast conclusions when facing a client's artwork or behavior. This happens because, while facing phenomena, we tend to look for fast and easy explanation formats, in order to minimize our anxiety in the presence of an unknown or obscure situation. When a person starts a process in which he tries to express artistically an idea, or when the person lets go of its mechanism of defense and yields to an artistic activity, he is occupied with an integration of cognitive, emotional, technical and creative elements. If the outcome is characterized by minimalizing the outcome, yet the outcome is very effective and impressive, then we must agree that the person has the talent to produce an outcome which overcomes the challenging obstacles he faced during the process. This is a testimony to skillfulness, zeal, efficiency, high potential for generalization and integration. However, this condensation can, at the same time, be reasoned due to defensive, manipulative motivation served as a disguise, yet can be attributed to talent if the motivation is decent. So, in conclusion, we need to analyze how the work was done and for what purpose.

The third possible proportion is *big dimension, but poor message*. Vast dimension may require excellent skills but can also indicate waste of material used for mere showiness or possible clumsiness. Vast dimension may be rooted in the client's need to sensationally impress the observer or himself. Big artworks require lots of materials, many musical instruments and powerful energy. The client is investing, producing, moving or playing, causing lots of noise, but finally he is not producing a message. Your impression is that the emphasis of the client is more on the senses and less on the intellectual impact, which can use the arts in order to reveal an idea. The style of dimension and sensation emphasis over idea is typical developmentally of young toddlers, who are joyful because they can act upon the material, rather than produce a story or content through a material's artistic tools.

The last possible outcome is an artistic production of *small dimension and poor message*. This is typical of mentally challenged or very depressed people. They don't have the psychic assets required to fruitfully advance along the Creation Axis. It shows a lack of Ego power, in the Jungian sense. In such cases we, the therapists or coaches, are expected to help the client arrive practically to an artistic product which will symbolize a feeing, idea, conflict or wish, in order for us to elaborate with the client on its emotional level.

All the artistic factors which I shall survey and analyze from now on belong to the "how" or "which" behaviors of the client while creating the arts – however, we shall look at them in depth, mainly in order to find indications as to what our client faces. Conflicts, drives, sexual desires, health and wealth issues, ethical dilemmas, fears, hopes and plans – all hide under those indicators.

Color/Form

K: You can also make diagnostic distinctions by comparing the ratio between *color* and *form* in the artwork. What do you mean by Color and Form? Are you talking about analyzing how colorful the artwork is?

A: When we arrive to Color and Form, we must paradoxically take under consideration that these factors obtain important hints about the client's unconscious and his or her personality traits.

Let me first relate to *Form*. Form derives from the cognitive mental source of the performer. By cognitive, I mean how the client organized the emotional idea into such a structure that the idea will be transmitted to the observer in an intentional motivation. As if the client states, through the artifact, that "This is how I want you to see or experience my artistic outcome." The way the client wants to present his art conveys his or her ability to put the various parts of the art together and integrate them into a one artistic entity.

Hans and Shulamit Kreitler (1972), in their important book *Psychology of the Arts*, present us with a profound survey based on research on Form and on Colors. When referring to *Form,* they base their statements on Kohler (1947) and Koffka (1935), the Gestalt Psychology masters. Form is a frame, they claim, which causes tension or relaxation in the observer. The Form possesses three qualities: (1) The *parts* of the Form which are organized as a *whole*, (2) Transposition – meaning the Form's parts can be changed in size, posture or direction, yet they preserve the Form in its original effect. For example, a square remains a square, even though it is sketched in pencil, ink, in red or black, even if it is small or big, and even if it is made out of sticks or engraved in stone. It's the same with music. A melody will remain the same melody, even if we changed the scale, and the dance will stay the same, even if it is slowed down or sped up. (3) The Form is causing the observer an experience located in a sequence between the two poles, the two opposing qualities: The "cohesive" quality, which strives for stability by diminishing the flow of energy to a minimum, and the "blocking" quality, which strives for a differentiation of the parts. They speak about "Good Form" which, according to Gestalt Psychology, means a Form which possesses the quality to bring the observer to the self-regulation of his internal and external calmness and homeostasis.

We must understand that the Form is causing the client and the observer (therapist or coach) an emotional impact, as a result of how it is organized and performed.

Let's relate now to Colors. As mentioned, the Kreitlers (1974) teach us that every art causes us either tension or repose. If we eliminate the content which the art bequeaths, we remain only with Form and Colors. Forms are made by the different hues between the different colors, though in daily life we got accustomed to perceiving the forms as basic representations of the world's structures and their significant meanings. However, from the sensational perception, the forms are nothing but derivates of the different hue contours. Kandinsky (1955) validated these phenomena by stating that "a drawing is nothing but an organization of colors." So, if Forms are merely a byproduct of existing colors, we should observe drawings and art products only from the colors and contents point of view. In the chapter on the psychology of colors, the Kreitlers (1974) present us with a survey on tension-relaxation color combinations, colors and meaning, free associations to colors, cultural influence on colors, color preferences, symbolism and archetypes in colors.

From these assumptions about colors, we may infer that colors strongly impact us psychologically. Researchers showed that, amongst all colors (including Black, which corresponds to White, which emphasizes the Black), it is Gray which causes relaxation. (Kreitler, 1974). Colorful art automatically evokes emotional responses. Using colors denotes high emotional involvement. If presented in good form, it proves that the feelings are well-organized intellectually.

K: What do you mean when you say "good form?"

A: Before I try to conceptualize what is bad or good form, let me share with you my motivation to be able to diagnose an art product as "good form" or "bad form." I enter this dilemma as a therapist, not as an art critic. A "good" formed art allows me to lean on the client's mental assets, when I consider an intervention, while a "bad" formed art will result in my planning an extra precaution towards a client with a testified vulnerable or undeveloped Ego, in the Jungian sense.

Form is a short term for formatted, formulated material. This art is formatted according to, and within, implicit aesthetic rules. A "good form" is a piece of art or movement or music which correlates to normative aesthetic rules. There are aesthetic rules that are derived from history and culture. So, a good form is a form which corresponds with the actual norm that exists where the client was raised or is living. If the artist deliberately breaks those aestetic rules, he or she creates a new dialogue and challenges him or herself and te observer with a new style.

Previously, we discussed the three basics which structure a good form (parts as a whole, transposition and cohesive vs. blocked dynamic), and now we can add that a norm, which corresponds to cultural aesthetic rules like perspective, figure and ground and symmetry will be considered as "good form." A bad form is any form that does not stick to these rules.

If we apply all the above to Expressive Arts Therapy and Coaching, we need to take under consideration the quality of the artistic performed art, the norm at a certain place and culture and judge promptly our therapeutic interventions.

K: How do you diagnose the proportions between *color and form*?

A: I observe the colors and I look at the hues, and I try to understand the meaning of the colors in relation to the form. Example: If the sculpture is a huge mass of undifferentiated clay covered by colorful glaze, I shall analyze how this colorful cover relates to the undifferentiated block of clay. In this case, both the form and colors are very primal, and this means the emotions expressed are primal, primitive and may display undifferentiated feelings. However, if the pile of clay is undifferentiated, yet the colors are painted in punctual strips, I can assume that, under his undifferentiated potential, there are organized emotions with the intention to be seen in proper order. So, what you can figure out from this way of diagnosis is that I train myself to understand the meaning I obtain from of these two factors: Color and form.

Each color can have numerous symbolic representations. Example: Let's take two colors, red and green, and see their symbolism in art.

Red: Based on research reported by Gegorian (1996) in *The Journal of Arts and Psychotherapy*, people who suffer a trauma unconsciously prefer to use black and red colors. Black for smoke and red for blood. People tend to choose red and black in order to express, fear, trauma and despair. In a piece of research I oversaw and reported in Goren-Bar (2000), titled "Children in Stress and in Emergencies," I analyzed drawings of adolescents who suffered severe trauma when two Israeli helicopters crashed near their high school yard. They, too, apparently preferred black and red colors to express the disaster they had gone through.

However, from a Jungian point of view E. Neumann (1971), in *Amor and Psyche*, explains that red signifies femininity: Women's life cycle is connected to bleeding. A woman gives birth through blood, she gets her period through blood, she blushes and becomes pale losing her blood, her internal sexual organs are pink – she is considered a "rose" and losing her virginity can be analogous to a rose bud which opens up. There for we shall consider attribute red to feminninity.

Green: Let's refer to the color green and try to follow my way of thinking. Green may connect to photosynthesis, a botanical process used by plants in which energy from sunlight is used to convert carbon dioxide and water into molecules needed for growth. This signifies transformation in nature, which results in growth connected to "Life." After I understand the symbolic representation of the color, I immediately ask myself: "How is this symbolic color presented in the artwork, and in which form is it presented?" Does the symbolism of the color suit the form by which it has been chosen to be performed? Are the feelings expressed through the colors arranged intellectually and cognitively? Does the Form contain the emotions properly or do the feelings burst out from the Form in an unorganized form, hinting at possible impulsiveness, aggression or maybe hysteria?

Let us be aware that Feelings/Colors expressed in a "bad form" may denote malignant issues. Feelings/Colors held in good form are benign, controlled and are adequately expressed and communicated.

K: I understand the importance of those criteria for the therapist's diagnostic thinking, however, don't you exaggerate in being too judgmental in hurrying up "diagnosing" the person's naïve artifacts?

A: Here again I paradoxically thank you for this comment. It is so important for me to stress, again and again, that all my diagnostic assumptions must first be evaluated based on the client's life story, the reason for his referral and complaints, and then be brought up as a dialogue, preferably during in the sixth phase of the Creation Axis, Preservation.

K: Can you give me an example of how you determine malignant from benign concerns to feelings?

A: Two boys start Expressive Therapy and both choose to draw with gouache colors. One child, who has behavior problems, enjoys splashing the colors, one on top of the other, and gradually these colors accumulate to become dirty gray blot. This is an example of using the feelings/colors in a very primal, spontaneous, uncontrolled form. The child expresses despair and aggression through his art. He doesn't care to differentiate between colors. What he is intrigued with are the kinetic splashes of the colors which emerge from the tube. You see that this child is still connected to the basic, primitive, primal feelings of aggression and impulse. He expresses life through basic sensory stimulation.

The other boy, the same age, comes to the same studio, takes up the same gouache colors and asks the therapist "Can I have a pallet for mixing colors?" He is taking the right amount required of each color. Some colors he mixes, so he takes the red and white and turns it into pink; he takes red and yellow and mixes them into orange. You see that he differentiates, processes to fit a feeling to color, sorting them out to express what needs to be revealed. He prepares a big color repertoire with which to express himself. Then he approaches the white canvas and makes a drawing. When you look at the drawing, you see it has good form. You can observe that there is an intercorrelation and interaction between components. Then you ask him "what did you do?" and he shares with you a certain explanation of content. He sublimates better, he is more sensitive and delicate with the way he expresses himself. I am not saying that the one child is good and the other is bad. I'm describing two styles, two motivations, two approaches to the same assignment.

Form vs. Content

Another important diagnostic source with which we can obtain data about our client is the comparison between *Form and Content*. Diagnostic data is obtained when you compare one dimension to another. If you compare male to female, you will find differential diagnosis – you will find that they have common features and others that are totally different. When we diagnose forms compared to content, you will glean four options.

K: We've already discussed what counts as good form, however, I have no idea what represents good content. Can you elaborate on that?

A: Prior to explaining to you what is considered "good content," let me share with you a recent experience I had with a successful businesswoman of forty-five, mother to a daughter of six who came to consult with me about her stubborn daughter and ended the session encountering her falling-apart marriage. I suggested she come up with an associated word which could summarize our session, and to which she will attach a drawing with pastel colors. She enthusiastically agreed, stated the word "Hope," referring to our agreement that she would do her very best to bring her husband to couple's therapy. Now I shall describe for you the drawing she did abruptly on an A4 page: On the bottom, she situated a sea or wide river colored blue, while on the upper side of the paper she drew blue clouds. Both the sea and clouds were painted with the same blue hue, not differentiating the water above from the water below. On the upper left side of the paper, behind a cloud, she drew a small sun with a few short rays. If we analyze her work according to "form" versus "content," we will agree that, considering her age and intellect, on the form level the work is regressive, undifferentiated, yet basically well-organized. However, on the content level, two main factors were either missing or undeveloped. The picture lacked ground representation, with no land nor use of brown color, and the sun was significantly diminished, extremely small. When I asked her what, in her opinion, was possibly missing in her drawing, she immediately responded "the earth and the sun are too small?" We discussed the significance of those basic missing factors and agreed that the small sun represented her reserved hope for significant change in her spouse's attitude. Thereafter, I advised her to invest in a possible "playground," a possible soil path to represent what she needs to do with her husband. What turned this into a very significant therapeutic experience was her artistic attempt to draw the brown path, report on upcoming obstacles, and realizing that couple's therapy will not be an easy path to a miracle.

We will consider "*good content*" under two conditions. First, when the client's story has a beginning, a process and an end. Second, when the client's testing of reality is fine. Testing of reality is the objective evaluation of an emotion or thought against real life, as a faculty present in normal individuals, but defective in psychotics. Reality testing is the psychotherapeutic function by which the objective or real world, and one's relationship to it, are reflected on and evaluated by the observer.

The story should present a coping Hero, a main character who competes with the challenging assignment. (The Hero does not necessarily need to be human or animal, it can be an object or a virtual entity or value, such as a story about "hope"). The main character embraces the journey. Conflicts, desires, wishes are expressed within the framework of the "good story." In the face of severe challenges, a person reacts through mechanisms of defense. A defense mechanism is an unconscious psychological mechanism that reduces anxiety arising from unacceptable or potentially harmful stimuli. Sometimes the defenses are effective, and other times they turn into pathology and damage the Hero quest. Defense mechanisms may result in healthy or unhealthy consequences, depending on the circumstances and frequency with which the mechanism is used. Hence, the content of the client's artistic production reveals his or her style of coping. If the mechanism of defense expressed in the content is functioning well, it will serve the client's coping. This shows "good content." Mind you, we are not expecting that the story be happy or pleasurable. The story can end with a murder, with death. But if the story makes sense, then this is a good content.

"Bad content" is the opposite, when the Hero is not coping with the assignment. In psychoanalytic theory, defense mechanisms are psychological strategies brought into play by the unconscious mind to manipulate, deny or distort reality, in order to defend against feelings of anxiety and unacceptable impulses, and to maintain one's self-schema. These processes that manipulate, deny or distort reality may include the following: Repression, or the burying of a painful feeling or thought from one's awareness, even though it may resurface in a symbolic form; identification, incorporating an object or thought into oneself; and rationalization, the justification of one's behavior and motivations by substituting "good" acceptable reasons for the actual motivations. The Hero feels out of control. If there is no logic connecting the sequence of the story, the content is probably bad. If the content reveals words without a significant message or meaning, it will be considered "bad content." If the consequences of the story are bad, malignant, and the defense mechanisms are weak, I shall be concerned about the client's coping mechanism.

K: I guess, then, we can get four distinctive cells again. What do they tell me?

A: When I share these options with you, they will open up options of interventions that illustrate how to relate to the artistic work the client has made, when considering the "story" he tells you in association with his artifact.

K: If I understand correctly, the therapist or coach is observing through the art what kind of person he is dealing with, and adjusts the therapeutic practice accordingly?

A: Yes, I make a distinction between 4 groups.

	+ Form -	
+ Content	Good form/ Good content	Bad form/ Good content
-	Good form/ Bad content	Bad form/ Bad content

When the form is good and the content is good–this shows a neurotic person. Like most people, the client has stress and contained emotions, but he can elaborate and tolerate them. These are the usual clients who attend our workshops. With such proportions, you may elaborate freely in the Elaboration phase of the Creation Axis.

K: What does it mean, diagnostically, if someone creates art with bad Form and good Content?

A: When the *Form is bad and the Content is good*, the subject probably has some kind of physical damage, handicap, like cerebral paralysis. In Expressive Therapy, it is advisable to help out the client on the logistical and organizational side of the artistic production (problems with the Form), in order to guide the handicapped client to the Main Theme in the Creation Axis, and benefit from the contents, which he can express well.

When the Form is bad and the Content is good it means that, intellectually and emotionally, the person is well-developed, but the way he transmits his idea into artistic media is poor. It may be because of objective handicaps, starting with physical or organic problems, hyperactive disorders, clumsiness or anxiety. We can differentiate various limitations through the client's proceedings along the Creation Axis.

K: How can a therapist help such a person? What is problematic here? Why not respect the client's limitations and stay with the bad form?

A: Because you are not an occupational therapist, but an Expressive therapist or coach, you have to help the client overcome his objective physical handicap, in order to enable him to arrive at the Main Theme. My message to such a client is: "We don't care how your work turns out, we care about your story and we shall express it!"

K: So, if I understand correctly, it's not about correcting the bad Form itself. It's about adjusting the therapy to his available Form, in order to complete the artistic process. It's mostly about providing him with the access to Expressive Arts so that the client can express his emotional and psychological problems.

A: Yes, you are right in this case, where the *form is bad and story is good*, I will compensate for the person's inadequacies. Bad form means that the client cannot, for various reasons, produce the art as it is expected, according to the norms of his culture. For example, he is handicapped after a car accident or post-operation. He cannot function well with his hands, he cannot see well, he cannot move about, he cannot pinch, etc. There is an objective obstacle that is distorting his Form quality.

In cases where both the Form is bad and the Content is also bad, I will help the client overcome his objective handicap, in order to arrive at a Main Theme (even though the Main Theme may be malignant). This means that on top of my therapeutic motivation stands the theatrical stage, the artistic-emotional expressivity and the way to achieve that, including my active assistance in bringing the idea into a realistic art performance, as "bad" as it may appear.

K: As I understand you, the therapist or coach should adjust the Expressive Arts therapeutic potential to the client, so that, eventually, the client will approximate the expectation of aesthetic Form. Our purpose is to arrive at his level, in order to help him, eventually or gradually in time, shift as closely as possible to the client with "good Form and good Content."

A: Yes and no. No, because mainly we want to elaborate on the content. Yes, because naturally a handicapped client eventually improves his or her artistic performances, the more he or she practices the Expressive Arts media.

K: I wonder, what is the type of intervention for a person who shows *Good Form but Bad Content*?

A: The artistic productions of the *Good Form - Bad Content* combination are typical of most people who attend therapy or coaching in crises. This combination is in the essence of Sublimation. The client comes to therapy in order to release his or her malignant content, and in Expressive Therapy & Coaching, this is done through the arts. The main asset which serves the client on his Expressive Therapeutic quest is creativity. The "bad story" is designed or expressed in an artistic manner.

The client usually presents a beautifully-formulated artwork, which may reveal terrible things. Such artworks contain secrets, perversions, traumas and all kinds of contradicting content which is connected to the client's shadow. While working with clients who present the combination of *Good Form-Bad Content*, we should be aware to their defense mechanisms, because the post-trauma and sufferings cause fear, and usually the mechanism of defense is not efficient, is dysfunctional yet, in other cases, it may be very rigid and defensive.

We need to pay attention to two phases in the process. The first phase: The client arrived at the Main Theme and laid down, in artistic Form, the malignant Content (because the content is traumatic and bad). Phase two: Having the malignant content in artistic form, we are expected to elaborate on it expressively, in order to bring the client to a state of relative relief or resolution.

A few more words on elaborating the expressed trauma. *Good Form and Bad Content* suggests a post-traumatic, or narcissistically-wounded, or borderline person. Their artistic expressions are adequate, but their story is unfortunate, calling for an "Object Relations approach" (see Chapter 5). With such cases, the Expressive Therapist is required to enable the client to befriend the trauma, put it upstage, sublimate it and turn the traumatic story into a meaningful strength.

K: The last one is *Bad Form and Bad Content*.

A: These are the psychotic clients or the terribly mentally challenged. They will produce bad artistic products in Form, along with very irrational Content.

The Expressive Therapist, in such cases, needs to reduce the artistic process to basic functioning, positioning the therapeutic challenge in terms of fundamental fragments of performance. We are required to help with the contact & organizational phases of the Creation Axis, in order to reach a reasonable Main Theme. We must avoid a judgmental approach to the irrational content and bring the client to an emotional resonance with the content. A small piece of art, a basic movement, a simple rhythmic bar attached to simple short sentences or even words, which highlight the emotional experience associated with the art.

K: Sorry to interrupt you, but I think this is a necessary question. How does an Expressive Therapist or Coach know the background of such a client? Do you extrapolate from the artistic piece or do you get it from the "Intake?"

A: I get basic information from the Intake, and I inquire as to why the client has been referred to me. Additional data comes from what I explained to you in the beginning of our diagnostic talks. We talked about the *norm*, what is expected of a person of that age and background, the *overt talents* of the client, meaning the here and now artistic repertoire, and the *future developed potential* which is embedded in the art. When I work with a post-traumatic person, I take under consideration the norm. A post-traumatic will bring forth the trauma as a story expressed in art. The overt is what I witness. I want to see it, I wish him or her to show it to me artistically. If the client denies the trauma, was raped and would not talk about it, would not display it in art, eventually we will arrive at the malevolent content. The potential hides under the word "sublimation," meaning how the client closes this dramatic gestalt? How does the client own this trauma? What does he learn from this accident or events and how does he or she take it as an advantage, in order to move on. In essence, how do you turn a shadow into power, and how does Expressive Therapy serve in this process of empowerment?

K: It's all about bringing the bad content into the light of meaning?

A: The therapist wants to turn the client's experience into a positive story. A positive story can also be a new and coping way to look at the trauma. Note that the therapist cannot dissolve the memories or the wounds of the trauma. The goal is to arrive at reconciliation, acceptance and meaning.

K: If I understand correctly, the clients who present *Good Form and Bad Content* are not that distant from the clients who present *Good Form and Good Content*. It's just harder for the therapist to translate the bad Content in a comprehensive, learning way.

A: Yes, somebody could go through a trauma and still create good Form with good Content. You can draw a line where, on one pole, there is *good Form/bad Content*, and on the other pole stands *good Form/good Content*, and the therapist's challenge is to turn, through Expressive Arts experiences, the bad Content into good Content, in the sense that the client learns to "own assertively" the bad Content and, by doing this, turns it into a good

Content, a life-challenging experience which the client turned, through therapy, into an empowered asset.

K: So, if I understand correctly, it's not about correcting the bad Form itself. It's about adjusting the therapy to the client's available Form, in order to complete the Expressive experience. It's mostly about accessing the Expressive Arts method within him, so that the client can express his emotional and psychological problems.

A: Yes, you are right, but you are missing two methodological points of view.

In this case, where the *Form is Bad and story/content is Good*, I will compensate for the person's inadequacies. You may remember the injured student without legs? I made the whole class crawl on the floor to enable him feel equal, and while using plastic art materials, I shall help the client achieve better Form, and in music I shall play for the client and accompany his poor singing.

K: The therapist should adjust the Expressive technique, compensate for the expected aesthetic form, in order to help the client, eventually or gradually, function expressively, just like a "normal" person. What is the right approach towards a person who shows good Form but bad Content?

A: Such traumatized clients will share with the therapist an unfortunate story in a very artistic manner. It's usually a beautifully-formulated artwork that reveals terrible things. Such artworks contain secrets, perversions, traumas and all kinds of morbid content which, in Jungian terms, belong to the domain of the Shadow archetype. Usually, the combination of good Form and bad Content means that the client suffers from dysfunctional defense mechanisms.

Because the Content is traumatic and "bad," we want, therapeutically, to elaborate on the Elaboration phase of the Creation Axis. Once the client beautifully sublimated the trauma through the arts, we want to elaborate on the main theme and benefit from intermodal therapeutic interventions.

I'll give you an example: I worked, many years ago, for the Ministry of Defense, in the Department of Casualties. They referred to me an adolescent who'd lost his father in the war. Unfortunately, that guy had been emotionally disturbed even prior to the loss of his father, and the "package" he brought to therapy was deeper and wider that the orphan experience he had undergone recently. He used to create art and sing terrible songs describing how desperate he was in life. In the Elaboration phase, in the presence of his artistic productions, I improvised melodies on the guitar which were based on his malignant texts. We used to invent songs together, connected to his artworks, and this Elaboration added comfort and containment to his desperate feelings.

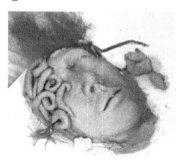

Diagnostic Thinking in Expressive Arts Therapy and Coaching

K: What about the client who expresses the art with bad Form and bad Content? What is significant about their art?

A: Bad Form and bad Content indicates a client whose cognitive functioning is deteriorating, followed by his deterioration in the way he approaches organizing, because "good Form" is the result of good organization.

An example in art therapy is a client who was hospitalized in a psychiatric clinic. In an art therapy session, he wishes to create a sculpture of himself (quite pretentious, I would say). He starts with the head and invests much energy and intention in creating his portrait (he forgot or gave up on the body), but the more he is invested in the details, the more he produces what looks like a monstrous animal. By focusing obsessively on each detail separately, he finds it impossible to put together the facial details appropriately, and the result is quite frightening. When asked to share a story about this artifact, a narrative is told which has nothing to do with the client. He is lost in associations caused by the difficult assignment he took upon himself. One could argue that I am being judgmental, and this is merely creativity or surrealism of some kind. Yet, the difference between creativity/surrealism and *"Bad Form"* lies in the quality of the "Form." In our case, the Form is bad, and any attribution of creativity or surrealism is a distortion of the artistic quality [2].

K: How do you approach such clients?

A: I put more emphasis on the Organization phase. When the client is so inadequate, it gives us a chance to establish a deep relationship with him, solely by investing in the Organizational phase. At the bottom of the Organizational phase lies an attempt on the therapist's side to adopt, adjust and shape the artistic environment to the client's needs, and to help the client sort out his or her preferences resulting from his or her limitations. All this communicative adjustment is purely an empathic experience (in Kohut's terms) and, therefore, is highly healing. Following the Organizational phase, I shall encourage the client to skip the Improvisation phase, in order to help him or her to arrive at and express the Main Theme.

K: Can you give me an example of how you skip the Improvisation phase, so I can imagine how the process takes place?

A: Skipping the Improvisation phase is not a fixed recommendation, when the client creates "bad" Form and "bad" or "good" Content. If your therapeutic impression suggests helping your client befriend the artistic material, it is better to establish playfulness and to dwell in the Improvisation phase, which merely

---

2 On Schizophrenic art you may read in my book Psychodynamic Snapshots in Expressive Arts Therapy coming soon in summer 2018 in Cambridge Pub house.

centers on the senses and on the manipulation of the artistic materials. But if you are therapeutically-oriented towards the *Content,* because we want to elaborate on the "story," we should help the client arrive at the Main Theme. If the client faces objective difficulties in making art, movement or music, we should skip the Improvisation phase and arrive directly at the Main Theme, by saying: "Let's try to create this idea of yours through music, art or movement."

K: So, you're very organized with such a client. Basically, you're teaching him or her to deal with the "Form." Because you're dealing with "Form," you're also creating rational and sensible Content.

A: As you can clearly note, these four options already offer a lot of diagnostic data. Mind you, it still deals only with "How" the client expresses himself with hints towards the Content that preoccupies the client.

K: We have not yet talked about diagnostic analysis of the client's Content. What is the meaning of the client's story?

Location, centers and focusing in a relationship to ensure balance and symmetry

A: One option to begin diagnosing the client's Content is by observing basic elements, such as the *location factor* in the artifact, the *existing center* of the performed art, and the *focusing element* in a relationship to ensure *balance and symmetry.*

K: Wow, that's a lot of "Content hints" to observe. Can you start by explaining what the location factor is?

A: *Location.* The location factor tells you where your client locates his intentions, and to which place he chooses to attribute the attention. Is it in the foreground of their artwork, which means it is on the conscious level of their awareness? What is located up front hints at the here and now relevancy of the Content to our client's everyday life. If the Main Theme is located on the horizon, it hints at a decision (either conscious or unconscious) to push away certain things into the background. We may attribute to the horizon or the background locations the quality of the unconscious. If the emphasis or intention of the client is headed towards the *right or left margins,* we may refer to several diagnostic options. Perhaps the client silently states: I see the object, but it's not at the center of my attention, or my awareness, though it exists. If it's located on the right side of the artistic production, we may assume that the object is connected with the brain and with cognitive thinking. If it is located on the left side, where the heart is and the font of emotions, we may refer to an object or an idea which preoccupies our client emotionally.

In a rectangular formed artwork, if the object is located in the center, the object cuts the rectangle into two triangles. Symbolism attributes femininity to the circle and square, and masculinity to the triangle. In such a case, it may be crucial to consider why the client possibly attributes masculine traits (in the Jungian sense) to the object selected to be located at that particular place. That crucial location creates a hidden tension between the two triangulated poles.

When I am "location-oriented," I say to myself: "Ah-ha, it is located in the upper register, so my client attributes 'supervision' to this object." Or: "Oh, this one is in the lower portion, so it's hiding or holds the whole structure above it." Or: "Ah-ha, this is on the right or on the left..." I always ask myself while observing "What is the significance of the location?"

K: What about "centers" and "focusing?" How is it different from location?

A: Location tells the observer where the client put what. When analyzing the "center" criteria, I examine the energy which magnetizes the objects around it. What is the anchor that gets the role of centering the "artistic event" and how does it connect the individual objects around it? Usually the "center" represents the "Ego," the "me," the central figure or object in the holistic experience. The center presents the most important part of the artwork. The part which connects all the components and holds them together. When I remove, in my imagination, the client's artistic center, I can imagine how weak the artifact becomes. If I take it away, I imagine how everything falls apart.

    Now here is the difference between "center" and "focus." Center is only one option that might hint at the client's intention of attributing importance to certain factors in his or her artwork. Focusing is a wide category which hints at the client's inner motivation during the Creation Axis. The client may be focusing on dimension (big/small); wishing mainly to impress, focusing on material and sensational experience; wishing mainly to enjoy the physical qualities of the artistic media, focusing on the content; busy mainly with the story and the text or the fable , focusing on the composition; mainly preoccupied in how to assemble the various parts into an integrated whole; focusing on the rhythm; mainly oriented towards the kinesthetic qualities of the experience; focusing on colors; driven mainly by emotions, etc. What I mean by focusing is where the clients invests his artistic energy and motivation. Each of the options I have mentioned here may tell us a lot about the focal point of the content with which our client is busy.

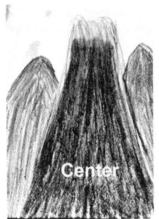 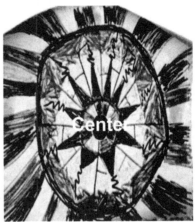

Focusing can also display our client's intentions through extra additions placed in the artistic creation. For example in the previous picture, The background of this surrealistic drawing called the attention of the artist to focus on the skeleton on the right margin.

K: What about *balancing* and *symmetry*. What does symmetry signify?

A: *Symmetry.* The client puts emphasis on symmetry for two reasons. The first indicates that the client is obsessed with justice. This item needs to be located equidistant to the other object, or on this side versus the other side. As if the client says: "If I do this, I will be fair enough, equating it with another thing. If you break the client's attempts at symmetry, you will break his balance of control. Symmetry bequeaths the client with harmony, sometimes a pseudo-harmony. It's an extension of the obsessive-compulsive need for justice or control. Remember the rule of 70%. If all movements, musical lines or artistic products are made or presented

symmetrically, it may hint at a certain rigidity.
There is another, deeper level of symmetry. This is the narcissistic need of the client to be seen in a *mirroring* manner. "Me" must be reflected in my other "me."

We shall witness, in a picture, a child opposing another symmetrical child, a tree facing a tree, a window facing a window, etc. In movement, one bodily expression repeats itself in a mirroring symmetrical kinesthetic expression.

In music, one musical sentence repeats itself in symmetry. On the one hand, these dual identical expressions give a harmonized feeling, yet their restricted repetition arrives at a certain boredom, as the repeated is already known and can be tedious.

K: Thank you for explaining this to me so thoroughly. I think we can proceed to the next method of content diagnosis.

A: *Integration.* The next factor includes all the previous elements we have mentioned so far and connects them into a single unit. That's why I call it "Integration." Integration tells me how the parts create the whole. How does a person bring several artistic elements together? Some clients achieve an integrative sensation to a drawing by adding a black contour, or line, which encompasses everything, others will squeeze together several items, and others use a passe-partout as background to bring together the parts into a whole. In movement, the client arrives at a Main Theme which includes all the various motions previously expressed in the dance, and in music the integration usually appears as a hymn or clear melody in which the listener can identify previous musical motifs which are integrated into the final heroic version.

As a diagnostician, you want to find the client's need for integration. A need for integration displays an intrinsic motivation for control, synthesis, harmony and closure. The Jungian sand tray is an excellent example of integration or disintegration. When people lay out miniatures on the sand, they may put them randomly, without any sign of integration or communication between the items. Others show an intrinsic need to connect the various items into a bonded interaction

 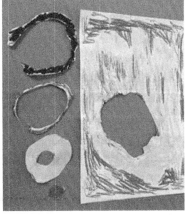

and, by this, retain a sense of integration. Usually within the integration we may identify internal differentiation: Who is more important, who is more submissive, who is marginal, who is in the center.

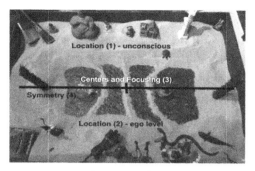

K: So, integration is that you follow the artistic process and you see how the client is moving or integrating everything together. You ask whether the integration makes sense? What is the emphasis the client is putting on certain parts of the art? Where is a specific component located, and how does it intercorrelate with the other components?

A: People create all kinds of art. They can dance, paint and play. At a certain moment, during the process of creating an artistic product, most people need to apply what I consider a "higher level of intellectual comprehension" to their art. This comprehension is displayed through the integration factor. Analyzing the "integrative factor" of an artwork provides clinical data about the client. It tells you a lot about the person. It shows the need of a person to organize his environment according to a proper inner organizational structure. Integration is a projection of an inner need, to create an artistic world in an organized form, according to an inner structure.

I'll give you a surprising example. If I enter my son's room and it is a mess, it means that he doesn't have any need for integration. He wakes up and leaves the bed, because for him the bed is the place where his body rests, simply a functional object (in Winnicottian terms, he merely relates to the object). When I wake up, I make my bed, because for me the bed is a symbol of a shrine. My inner structure of integrating (in Winnicottian terms) my bedroom is that I "use it" and see it aesthetically. My clinical experience shows that, when a person is mentally disturbed, the level of integration factors in his life are low and, by definition, his artistic productions are dis-integrated. Psychosis is called disintegration of the personality. Integration is an inner higher need to arrange components and fragments into a structure. The elevated psychic integration, according to C.G. Jung, is the Mandala.

K: You mentioned that Integration contains the previous factors we looked at, but can you explain the difference between Location, Centers, Focusing, Symmetry and Integration?

A: If you look at the same very picture shown above, what creates the integration in the picture is the white background made of the sand in the tray. The sand connects all the items and turns them into an imaginative basketball field.

K: I think I'm ready to progress to the next method of content diagnosis. What is it?

A: *Use of material.* Another method is to observe the *use and choice of the material*. The use of material relates to the artistic primal substance with which the client will create an artifact. When I say material, I don't necessarily mean art material only. In movement, space can be material, the upper or lower torso is material, using a scarf, a ball, and ropes are material. Relating to the other dancer in the space is material. Relating to the walls is material. In music a scale and a rhythmic bar are materials, and so is the choice of instrument. I ask myself questions like: "How is the client using the material?" "What sort of material he is picking up?" Each kind of material presents a psychic need and a psychic value.

Cotton may present a need for tenderness; metal a need for strength and statement; wood may present warmth and connectedness; "depth" may present unconsciousness and curiosity; darkness might be fear and the unknown; a trumpet's sound may present glory and triumph; a shout may present a call for help or protest. You can be definite about the client's psychic attribution to the material by simply validating your observation with the client's explanation for why he or she has chosen that kind of material.

The same goes for the choice of techniques applied. Tying or gluing may point at a need for bonding; pinching for a need to express aggression, jumping may hint at a need for detachment; cutting at a need for separation; staccato music may be chosen as technique for expressing joy, for sharpness and individuality, while legato may denote dependency, flow and tenderness. If the technique is surprisingly sophisticated, you can see that the client is using his intelligence to create solutions for challenging materials. This can refer also to life, meaning the client is a trickster and, by using all kinds of technical manipulations, he will invent creative solutions.

Now onto *directions and motion and intervals.* Another very important analytical factor is *direction* and motion. You see, if you're right-handed and you draw a line on the page, usually you will move your hand from left to right. You locate your hand on the left side of the page and, while moving right, you open a space where the line will be spread horizontally. Psychologically speaking, this "accordion" movement opens up air, shows established your existence as if the created line says: I was a dot and I can spread out and become a million dots – I became a line! The psychological sensation is expansion. When you're right-handed, and you draw a line from right to left, you will feel restricted and forced, as if you sucked the air in. Psychologically, you feel shrunk and restricted. So, psychologically speaking, "direction" embodies intention, hope, and is followed by breathing air. I am situated at a certain point and I head on towards my targeted destination, on the canvas, in space and on a musical scale.

I shall give you examples of the psychological intention the direction denotes. The direction, whether it comes from up-to-down (depression, yielding, giving up) or from down-to-up (emerging, growing, bursting), if it's circulating (inwards, meaning retroflection and introverting, if outwards means expanding and developing) or diagonally-directed (meaning splitting, cutting, changing direction, looking for alternatives). It's the same in the Jungian sand tray, asking how the client locates the miniatures and aimed in which direction. This will display the client's unconscious intentions.

Now let's speak about "*Motions*." I wish to remind you of when we spoke about emotions in Chapter One. We mentioned that ex-motion, meaning bringing motion outwards, means displaying feelings. If the motion is fast, it denotes high energy, the need for expansion, the need for achievement and appearance. Yet, if the motion is slow, it may display a need for meditation, introspection, hesitation, search, examination and exploration.

Intervals between items will hint at the intention the client places on certain items, as compared to other items. Symmetrical intervals will display respect and equality, whereas a large interval means separateness, isolation or potential space for additional options to appear.

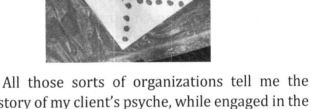

All those sorts of organizations tell me the hidden story of my client's psyche, while engaged in the artistic performance.

K: Are the other methods similar to these?

A: Let's look at *Quality of Line*. The same methodology applies to the Quality of the Line. When you produce art, you produce lines. You can produce it with a brush, a pencil, an etching. But in movement, also, we speak about the dancer's kinesthetic line or the melodic line. As I mentioned before, the quality of the line corresponds to the amount of air the client takes in, with the intention to exhale it through an artistic gesture. If the line has homogenous flow, it shows control and skillfulness.

If the quality of the line is fractured or denotes hesitation, it may mean suffering or uncertainty. We should heed the beginning and end of the line. Usually in the beginning of a created line, it displays energy (a thick amount of paint, strong energetic kinetics, high pitch and volume in music). At the end of the line, the energy fades away (exhaustion, giving up, shame, bashfulness). In order to have the same quality of line, no matter how long it endures, the client needs to invest the same energy throughout the line. It's the same with the sound of the uttered voice or melody, the same with movement in a dance. It tells me so much about the client's ability to spontaneously plan the targeted intention while performing. Is he hesitant, does he display low self-esteem, does he express modesty or pride, impudence or certainty? I look at the quality of the bent or the stretched limb, or the quality of the voice, and this gives me ideas for optional interventions later on, because I understand that the psyche is expressing itself throughout the line.

K: Sorry, but I don't think you explained this clearly

enough to me. You said, it gives you certain ideas about how the psyche is expressed, but that doesn't provide me with creative diagnostic thought. Can you elaborate?

A: When you are afraid, when you are fearful, your expressed lines will be short, troubled and shaky. This results from lack of air. While explaining this to you, I realize how often I say to my clients: "Breathe! Breathe well." I shall share with you a personal experience I had with my dog, Yoko. We often ride on my bicycle along the beach. She is on a leash, running parallel to me. Lately, I realized that, when I ride, there are occasions when I am suddenly surprised, and therefore anxious. Somebody may pass by too quickly with a bicycle, and this will cause Yoko to stop, and I may fall, so I become stressed. Or if I see somebody with a big dog ahead of me, I predict a potential dog fight, so I slow down or even stop but, paradoxically, my stopping calls for interaction, so I have to calculate whether it's better to stop or to continue. All this creates anxiety in me. I discovered that, when I breathe, I overcome those tiny crises. So, I take a deep breath of air, another one, and I move on. If I pass and nothing happens, I regain my normal breathing. I discovered that the length of the air gives me extra emotional power to overcome challenges. It's the same with the line. The line is an indicator of the inner energy the client can express in the presence of a threatening stimulus.

K: If you make small lines, you are conserving, keeping to yourself, you don't feel comfortable enough with your energetic effort to expand your artistic production. The therapist's role is to focus on how much energy is invested. The more energy invested means the more courageous the person, although they can be too courageous. Does it work like this?

A: Quality of the line is a hint that you have to look through in order to see whether there is a flow or a break, whether they are withholding or flowing.

K: On to *Prototypes*. We mentioned prototypes making their presence in the third, Improvisation phase of the Creation Axis. Isn't a line also a sort of a prototype? I'm eager to know more about prototypes, as I feel they hold a lot of diagnostic information. Can you explain more about them?

A: I am asked what is the difference between "Component" and "Prototype" in an artistic work? Well, then every piece of art (plastic, movement and music) can be differentiated into three parts. You may look at it as a Babushka (Matriyoshka, stacking Russian dolls) structure: The art as a whole, its components and its prototypes. Let us analyze the artwork from its smallest atom to the whole assembly (from prototype to Main Theme).

A prototype is an atom of energy embedded in an artistic expression. In the dictionary, it is defined as "an early sample, model, or release of a product built to test a concept or process, or to act as a thing to be replicated or learned from. A prototype is generally used to evaluate a new design, to enhance precision by system analysts and users. The word 'prototype' derives from the Greek πρωτότυπον prototypon, 'primitive form'... from πρῶτος protos, 'first' and τύπος typos, 'impression.'" Please notice that the Greek intention to emphasize in this concept is the primitive and original aspects of the word, denoting primal, original and spontaneous traits. In Object Relations psychology, these refer to the authentic, "True Self" productions. I claim that, in Expressive Arts Therapy, all the above means that the client may produce small spontaneous authentic graphical signs, movements and sounds which are mainly primal original gestures, and these may be changed or modified along the Creation Axis, to be developed into a Main Theme which is a much more elaborated version of the prototypes which were produced earlier in the Improvisation phase.

So prototypes are primal, original, spontaneous, tiny signs which tell us essential data about the client's basic, non-elaborated psychic energies, expressed in his artistic expressivity. Those prototypal signs, if we decipher their psycho-energetic qualities, can tell us crucial data about our client's aggression, tenderness, aspirations, inhibitions and needs.

An artwork can be very rich and expressive, even if it is only based on one prototype. This depends on the technique, composition, organization and energy discrepancies the client uses and operates on the artistic prototype. However, an artwork which contains a few prototypes can also be impressive, it all depends on the way the client is using the artistic prototypes in the framework of the whole art piece.

When the prototypes are organized in the art

as a "whole combined composition," they create the "Components."

The dictionary defines "component" as: "The constituents of a system. A part or element of a larger whole, a piece, an element, ingredient, building block, unit, module, section." In Gestalt Arts Therapy, when the client is asked to calculate the parts of his whole artwork (in order to hold a dialogue between them), he naturally refers to the components. Those components contain either one prototype or a few. It is of therapeutic importance to note how the prototypes are used or organized differently in each of the components, as this modification can hint at the psychological meaning of the hidden intention of the artist/client.

Here are several examples:

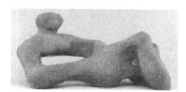

One prototype (smooth surfaces), 5 components: Head, breast, pelvis, limbs, empty space.

One prototype (strokes of a brush), 3 components: Cold colors, hot colors and a white area

3 prototypes (yellow smeared surface, tiny brush strokes some of which create flowers, others leaves, black thin long lines which create the branches)
5 components (tree 1, tree 2, flowers, black grass, yellow background)

5 prototypes (smooth surface, black holes, thin line scratches, curls, "pasta" snakes), 2 components: Hair, face

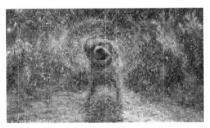

1 prototype (dots), 5 components: Twisting head, body, light blue aura, path, background

2 prototypes (brush strokes, black contour lines), 7 components: Trees, sun, stars, clouds, mountains, town, light yellow/white line above mountains

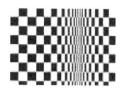

1 prototype (black/white square) 3 components: Left, middle, right

When we observe a readymade artwork, we observe first the Main Theme. The Main Theme can then be analyzed through its components, and the components are made of prototypes. The Theme in art is the final drawing or sculpture or video art, in movement it is the whole dance, in music it is the melody, song or instrumental piece. The client decides what the theme is. The therapist can ask the client: "What are you aware of?" "Can you give a name or a title to what you have just created or experienced?" The title will be the theme. The components are the different details which create the Theme. So, we can conclude that *Prototypes* are the client's psychic primal dictionary, which set up his artistic style. This is the artistic vocabulary of the client. It's that artistic gesture which can be differentiated through the energy that is expressed in a very small detail.

    The energy of the client, as expressed through the prototypes, serves as a sign for the coach or therapist. People discharge their energies as a function of either psychic and emotional responses to external life situations or as transmitters of internal stresses and needs. Simply, I can state: *Look at the prototype, analyze its physical traits and you will get a sample of your client's conscious or unconscious basic needs.* Another way to look at the prototypes is to consider them as the results of the client's *"artistic blood test."* Differentiating the client's prototypes will grant you an essential database for future interventions. Often, depressive people will function artistically through one prototype only. The more depressive, the fewer prototypes. But on the other hand. a piece of art can be very rich despite only having one prototype. For example, Pointillism is an artistic style expressed only through one prototype: The dot. (Remember the example of the wet dog above.) So, they express everything through one prototype, but what compensated and enriched Pointillist art was the extent of high expressivity, the variety of colors and the composition, otherwise it would have been dull and schematic.

K: Can you specify more about the psycho-dynamic meaning of the various prototypes which present different sorts of energetic graphical or movement or musical gestures?

A: Well, you certainly are challenging me to go quite deep now. Let's analyze this classical line called "Zigzag"

In order to create such graphical or kinesthetic movements or sharp sounds which repeat themselves endlessly in form yet change direction to 30 degrees opposite where it had arrived from, one has to invest sharp and fast energetic expressions, yet under fantastic control, as the lines have to be equal in length, strength and direction. Somehow, all these preliminary conditions are made easily and spontaneously, and this is what makes the analysis so challenging. From a diagnostic point of view, you have to slow down the manifestation in your head and trace the psychodynamic process which underlies such an artistic gesture.

Zigzag is supposing a funny, humorous repetitive artistic prototype, causing psychologically an impression of clumsiness, uneasiness, like a Charlie Chaplin walk, a drunk or a toddler's toddle, yet by analyzing the energetic investment of this prototype, you can find out it is a controlled, aggressive repetition which breaks the continuous flowing line and shakes the flow into many repetitive fractions.

Now, symbolically you may see the Zigzag line as aggressive, as it is associated with the sharp teeth of an animal or the teeth of a saw. The fluctuation towards one direction with immediate retreat back to where the movement started may symbolize a strong ambivalence: Yes and no, in and out, dare and regret.

So, if you follow my way of analyzing the prototype, *I first analyze its energetic and physical traits and then associate those traits with psychological qualities.* I translate into words the psychodynamic qualities of the graphical or movement or musical form and translate those qualities into psychological options which may fit the client's intention. In movement, for example, I ask myself why she would dance in this way, give and take, give and take, head upward-head downwards, up-down, open and immediately closed, again and again. If you open, why can't you stay opened? Why do you have to close immediately? I am dialoging with the prototypal form and I ask it what it possibly represents. Obviously, this ability of mine to dialogue with the prototypal form in my head enables me to join in with my client in this diagnostic search. Usually, the client will contribute better interpretations to the prototypal forms. I will always check my assumptions with my client. Does it make sense to him or her? After deciphering the symbolic meaning of the prototype, we can practice variations on the prototype. For example, I can encourage the "Zigzag client" to extend an arm, but instead of retracting it right away, to stay open and expand the openness, then check the psychological effect of breaking the prototypal Zigzag form and turning it into a flowing line. There, in the difference between the spontaneous authentic prototype (Zigzag) and the opposite "anti-prototype" (flowing line), lies the therapeutic insight.

K: Please present me with several more basic prototypes that I may find in a client's artworks. I think a few more examples will help me grasp your way of analysis.

A: Maybe I should try summarizing your request in a table form:

Name of pro-totype	Form	Physical energetic trait	Psychodynamic possible interpretation
Circle		Requires special perception, with basic potential for a good quality line, the upper half must correspond identically to its lower half. The total assignment requires same investment of energy.	A need to encapsulate, a feminine expression due to its roundish trait, a basic form resembles to human head, a container.
line		A graphical sequence requires the same investment of energetic air for length and width.	Border, basic infrastructure basis enabling direction, structure, division. Displays basic attempt at a start.
curve		A line changing direction may display rising energy, if turned upwards or losing energy, if directed downwards. If repeated, will cause a wave-effect.	A need for containment, in sequence may display tenderness and easy flow, is a variation on a half-circle.

spiral		Energy flowing either from inside out (growth) or from outside inward (retroflection).	Symbolizes the flow of life from birth to death or reversed. A meditative form, due to its symmetrical repetition.
dot		Strong energy condensed, controlled and directed at a small surface area.	An expression of coquettish decoration, skin presentation, symbol for a plentiful existence which may be easily produced, meditative, easy-going repetition which may hint at aggression.
ridge		Strong opposing energy which causes change on the flat surface.	An attempt to obtain three-dimensional effects, a technique causing a feeling of tightness and stickiness, aggression and individuality.

smooth		An effect caused by repetitive gentle, wet, circulating motions.	Symbolizes perfection, calmness, virginity. Space with potential for new emerging realities.

I am looking at the repertoire the client is using through graphical signs and gestures which creates his language of expressivity. It's the same in movement. A curve is a prototype, an abrupt limb extension is a prototype, a twist is a prototype and those prototypes hold psychic and psychosomatic knowledge. Everything that is squeezed, condensed or bent has psychological meaning. It may invite us to investigate psychic options, such as suppression, fear, hesitation, withdrawal or humiliation. All which demonstrates expansion, straight lines, one flow of homogenous energy, which expands equally, may correspond with freedom, independence and assertiveness. All which turns inward in a circulating form may refer to meditation and retroflection. All which expands towards the external world may refer to exploration, curiosity and a need for interaction.

I am tracing the energy and I'm translating the energy into a psychological hypothesis. I am not judgemental, and I measure my impressions upon the rule of 70%.

In my opinion, the prototype corresponds with the "Secret." In so many hours of intensive Expressive Arts seminars, workshops and individual sessions, I found again and again that the "Secret" hides in the small marginal details, and those are located in the prototypes. Only the prototypes can give us the hidden psychological intention of the expressivity.

K: Is it because we don't notice the details and avoid Focusing?

A: This is a crucial question and I thank you for it. Expressive Arts Therapy and Coaching becomes "clinical" if it dives psycho-dynamically into the details. Unfortunately, most Expressive Arts methods stay on the surface of the experience and avoid depth.

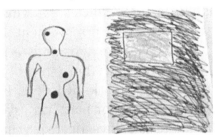

They leave the arts to affect the client and welcome the immediate experience. I wish to encourage the reader to dive in, to focus on the prototypes and decipher the marginal aspects of the artistic activity where the "Secret" dwells. Mostly, we are dealing with energy, how the energy is expressed.

K: I have a drawing a client of mine made. Maybe I can learn if you analyze it and explain the diagnostic thought behind it? Can we summarize all you have explained up until now?

A: In the drawing you present to me, we can count two main components: The white (the left side of the drawing) and the black (on the right side of the drawing). There are several more components: On the left side, we see the human-like figure as a component and the black dots make another component. On the right side, the gray frame is a component and the black scribbling another component.

What can we learn on the component level? We can learn that the client describes two realities. The white component shows a feminine figure with four black dots. Is this a disease? Or bullet holes? The lower part of the figure is missing, as if she cannot stand, without a base, and the contour is left opened on the knee lines. We do not see facial signs, which leave the figure anonymous, in a vulnerable state. The right side brings a component which transmits fast energy, chaotic lines, terrible noise. On the upper third of the component, we see a frame in a light color (another component), and sixteen faded circles can be vaguely seen inside. Does the right side of the drawing give emotional echo to the left, wounded side? All together we can count 7 components in the drawing.

What about the prototypes? First is a strong, clean and certain line, meaning that I am trying to appear and present myself. However, it is disrupted by the second component – a stressed line, a repetition of an existing line. This prototype means an imprint, a need to repeat a certain area of the existing line, strengthening certain places along the body. Meaning "my shoulders, my hips, my brain are important." The black dots are also a prototype, concentrating strong energy on a small surface and causing the effect of a wound or a disease. The next prototype is the Zigzag, which repeats itself endlessly on the right-side, black component. The Zigzag prototype displays here an emotional tempest which compensates the white wounded alien which has no facial features, and therefore cannot express its vulnerability or horror. Inside the white window, we observe the next prototype: Repeated curves. They are duplicated and made abruptly, opening several options: Are there more aliens outside? Are these cells which grow like bubbles?

You see that the prototypes add deeper emotional statements to the components. The "story" turns into real suffering, if we collect all the possible options the prototypes bequeath. Indeed, this drawing was made by a client who found it very difficult to report on her fear of sickness.

Chronology of acts

K: I realized, when I showed you the previous drawing, that you asked me which component had been drawn first, the right or the left side. You claimed the bright side was made first, and I confirmed your assumption. Why is the chronology of the artistic process important?

A: Chronology correlates directly with our discussion about the "process'" in Chapter One. The analysis of the *chronology* of acts may also reveal added valuable data to your diagnostic thought. Any art production is born through a process, whether it is a melody, dance or art. There is a beginning, continuation and an end. There is a dimension of time sequence, and what was laid down first, second and so on, what was first performed and into what was it developed is essential to the comprehension of the client's artifact. When I diagnose, I am interested, archeologically, in previous stages of the Creation Axis. How did it all start? What was the continuation, what happened next? What was in the finales? What did he or she do a moment before they presented the work to me or the group? The time dimension tells us a lot about the client's spontaneity, about the client's need for a basic, fundamental basis. The beginning creates a basis for the next occurrence – in order to start, you have to put your art material on a base that will later hold up the whole structure. How much planning is invested at the beginning? I follow the decision-making of the client throughout the process.

There are two points of historical observation: One is while the client actually performs. The second is in perspective, when the supervisee brings the client's work to supervision, or when we analyze the experience from a time perspective. Do notice if the client has regretted and changed something while at work. Note to yourself: Here he simplified, here he added, here he destroyed and made it much better. I want to know the story of the time sequence of the creation of the artwork. What do all those details contribute to our understanding of the client's performance and the psychodynamic behind it? The chronology opens a fan of data referring to the decision-making, the conflict to reveal, the drives of destruction, the ambition and inhibitions of the client, the need to hide and the need to expose, the giving up on attempts and the obstinacy to declare authenticity.

Contradictions

K: You also mentioned that the drawing I presented to you has a strong contradiction between the white side and the black side. Can you elaborate on the contradiction criteria in diagnosis?

A: Human beings' personality encompasses co-existing contradictions. I always remember, when reading the personal diary of Franz Stangl (Gitta Sereny, 1974), who was commandant of the Treblinka concentration camp, I was shocked how that murderer who was in charge of killing masses of people each day had cried when a canary died in his birdcage.

In the domain of *Contradictions, Ambivalence and Polarities* (see the chapter on Gestalt) we may find hints in the performed art which can give us ideas about the client's inner life. If you remember the last drawing we analyzed above, the contradiction between the left white side of the drawing opposing the black scribble reveals an inner conflict between the vulnerable side of the client's personality and its assertive opposing side. Contradictions inform you about psychic information which the client needs for compensation and complementary[3] experiences. Contradictions show you how expanded the client's personality is. I can be evil and I can be kind. I can be brutal and I can be compassionate. I can use a small amount of material but, at the same time, in another aspect of my work, I allow myself a horn of plenty and I can use a lot.

Also, always count how many contradictions prevail in a single artifact. When it's full of contradictions,

---

3 You may read about the compensatory function in Chapter 4.

it may display a state of mind where the person is ambivalent and cannot make up his mind. When there are several contradictions in the same artifact, it means that the person holds opposing needs, opposing interests, double-binded ideas and contradicted feelings.

K: Can you give me an example?

A: A woman created a sand tray which showed a landscape. On the right side of the tray, she located a sun and on the left side, a moon. So, this is a contradiction: Is it morning or night? From a Jungian aspect, if it's the sun then it's a masculine symbol, if it's the moon then it's feminine. Does she have a problem with her gender identity? Does she have a problem with her masculinity or femininity? Another contradiction was seen in the relationships between animals and humans: Apparently, it was the animals who fed the humans. And another contradiction was seen, where the house she located at the background was kept empty, and the furniture was beautifully arranged outdoors, in the front. When I asked for her explanation, she said: "This is my life, this is how I see it." We have here an example of "good Form" with "bad Content."

Another example which comes to mind is of a young client, age 32, whose sister and family had a car accident in which she died, and her family was injured. When he worked in a workshop and related to that recent tragedy, he asked to dance with music which he chose: Madonna's "Open My Heart to Me Baby." Facing our shocking response, he seriously explained that "the show must go on."

Investment of Energy

K: Now you ask me to relate to the investment of energy. Why so?

A: I also measure the investment of energy and gaps of energy within the artifact. Investment of energy means where the client puts more effort in making the art. If you observe a sequence of movement the client performs, you may notice that there are lapses, an increase in energetic movements and a relapse of energy which causes different emotional effects on the performer and on the observer. What is the hidden motivation for the distribution of energy within a movement scene? It's the same in music or art. The investment of energy displays attention and intention. More energy, more investment, more stress and more expressivity. Less energy causes repose and tranquility. The client is talking through the alterations of energies, and we want to trace his intentions.

K: Are there any more diagnostic criteria which lead you in your diagnostic thinking?

A: Yes, two more. One is the client's analytic approach.

Analytic Approach, Disseminating Systematically

An analytic approach, or "disseminating systematically," means that the client, while doing the art, analyzes it and says to himself: "I have to draw a person. It has to have a head. The head looks like a circle." Once the head is done, he goes on creating according to an inner inventory. "Two eyes, one nose, two ears," etc. He is registering the details and goes systematically by analyzing the expected object. We see such an approach when a rigid and inhibited person starts dancing, counting the steps, or when a person plays and sticks to the notes, eliminating a musical flow which allows emotional expressivity. The opposite performing style is the intuitive, creative client who goes with the expression and neglect details. I am differentiating between the analytic approach versus the expressive approach. The analytic needs control and forces cognitive considerations on the artistic assignment, while the holistic and expressive client connects to his feeling and improvises easily.

K: What is the last criteria?

A: This last criteria I learned from Dr. Itamar Levy, a psychoanalyst and art critic from Israel. In his unpublished article about Rembrandt, called "Decoration, Impersonation and the Denial of Depth," he distinguished between two artistic approaches: Anal and Genital. He claimed that the observer needs and can enjoy from both anal and genital art, and where anal is parallel or synonymous to "lots of," and genital denotes "few of."

When the client involves, in his artistic production, a lot of condensed artistic material, we may claim his style is Anal. The emphasis is on the quantity. Anal is an expression taken from Freud, and it relates to the anal stage, which is the second stage in Sigmund Freud's theory of psychosexual development, lasting from age 18 months to three years. According to Freud, the anus is the primary erogenous zone and pleasure is derived from controlling bladder and bowel movement. The major characteristic of this stage is the child's desire to collect, keep and hold property in his possession. By the same token, we can identify a need in the client's motivation to express his artifact with loads of materials. Usually, this kind of art is very decorative, because it has many repetitive elements. It does not express too deep a content, if any at all, but it will be very beautiful, because of the colorful, repetitive patterns.

The opposite is the genital art. Again, taken from Freud, this is the last stage of Freud's psychosexual theory of personality development, and begins in puberty. It is a time of adolescent sexual experimentation, the successful resolution of which is settling down in a loving one-to-one relationship. Sexual instinct is directed to heterosexual pleasure, rather than self-pleasure, as it was during the phallic stage. In art, the emphasis is on the message which is transmitted out front, erected with an idea or provocation which will call the observer's attention. The client artifact does not intend to please the observer, but rather is simple, blunt, condensed with very few material components, almost always just one, but the message is very strong and bursts out. It hits you. Giacometti's works can be considered genital art, while Bosch can be considered anal.

K: What is the significance of anal, and what is the significance of genital?

A: Anal is based on repetition. You use more of the same. Anal has an accumulative style. One layer on top of the other. Anal means there is a lot of variety in the artifact, colors, lines and materials. When observing anal work, you may feel suffocated or delight or stunned, as the art is loaded. Clients who demonstrate art in an anal style are overwhelmed. Often the personality is narcissistic and wishes to impress. Other times the anal art shows obsession, as the details are organized in endless order, there is a need for control, the client encompasses everything that is possible, doesn't give any space for the other.

Anal and genital artistic styles correspond to the horizontal and the vertical. Horizontal is when the art is telling you a story: You look at it and see that there is a beginning and an end. Vertical stands like a totem, like the Statue of Liberty. It presents a statement. In any piece of art, you may identify both qualities. One is genital and one is anal. The anal part in an art piece gives the observer a certain calmness, because artistic items are repeating themselves and grant the observer a sense of control, déjà-vu, a befriended reality. The genital relates to the anal as figure to background, in order to stand up front, ahead of the background, and call for the observer's attention to declare its message. Salvador Dali did this after the Second World War, when people melted in Hiroshima. This is a protest and, in this sense, it is a genital message, wrapped in anal decoration.

K: Taking for granted now my ability to differentiate between anal and genital styles, how do I benefit from this observation when practicing Expressive Therapy?

A: Let's start with the easy part, the genital art. Obviously, in this case, the client states clearly, through his or her artistic performance, the need to declare, express and share his or her argument. The Main Theme is clear, and we may go on elaborating on it (See Chapter 2).

The challenge, as I see it, is in the presence of anal art. Here we have to try to penetrate the decorative mechanism of defense, hoping to discover the genital factor hidden in the art. The client usually invests pure intention and efforts to create the artistic product. I am not sure that the client is aware that his or her invested, beautiful art is made as an artistic disguise. This is the challenge. The client is pleased with his work and happily wishes to work with it, to show it to others. However, as enthusiastically as he or she is to present their work, they are also withdrawn and suspicious about diving into their work and digging into its deeper layers. At that point, we need to be sensitive, cautious and, at times, determined.

Let's take a look first at movement therapy. Often, we see clients who prefer to dance when accompanied by music. Dancing, in itself, is blessed, ventilates, brings up emotions and, at the same time, can raise up negative emotions, as well (such as sorrow, longing and defeat). However, the client is not "dancing up a storm" I refer here to authentic movement, where the kinesthetic movement serves as a surfboard on which the client expresses *authentic movement*[4] material with which he later can associate and arrive at insight. In authentic movement, the client moves with eyes closed, which assures that the movement is not meant to impress, and therefore is, by definition, genital, it goes deep. However, even in a routine movement or dance, we should look at the prototypes and try to find that movement prototype which holds, for the client, an unconscious genital message. This is the "Secret." The genital artifact is an actualization of a genital message.

In plastic art, the picture is easier. Usually the anal art covers a hidden graphical genital agenda, which is the infrastructure of the whole mass of materials[5] lying one on top of the other. Using the principle of "chronology" in the artistic process, we can encourage the client to follow, step-by-step, what he or she has made, and discover at which point hides a charged feeling, idea or memory. Then, I use the Gestalt principle of "figure and ground," I refer to the plentitude of artistic materials as

---

4 Authentic Movement is an expressive improvisational movement practice that allows a group of participants a type of free association of the body. It was started by Mary Starks Whitehouse in the 1950s as "movement in depth."

"ground" and focus on the component which contains the "Secret."

K: The background of this picture is anal and the man in the front is genital?

A: The genital element here is obviously the screaming figure. The anal dimension appears as background made through two prototypes: Straight lines, which stand for the bridge, and endless curves, which stand for the mood. Now the genius, Munch, uses the same prototypes taken from the right side of the landscape and creates the genital figure from them. By this, he mixes the surroundings with the screaming figure, meaning the desperation is not only in me, it is wrapping me and the world.

References

Furth, G. (1988) The Secret World of Drawing, Healing through Art. Sigo Press, Boston.

Kreitler, H. & Kreitler, S. (1972) Psychology of the Arts, Duke University Press.

Kohler,W. (1947). Gestalt Psychology, N.Y. Liveright Publishing Corp.

Koffka, K. (1935) Principles of Gestalt Psychology. New York: Harcourt, Brace.

Neumann, E. (1971) Amor n, Psyche Mythos Books.

Chapter 7

Epilogue

Epilogue

It was Kristjan's idea to seal the book with a comprehensive case study which would integrate the vast knowledge we have described in length. Throughout the book, you came across numerous vignettes intended to illustrate theoretical arguments. This time, we thought it would be advisable to present a single longitudinal Arts Therapies and Coaching process, following several sessions. The day I emailed the chapter on diagnostics to our editor, I saw a client who came in to consult with me about a life crisis he was going through. Followed the Intake, I thought that sampling several sessions from his short-term therapy might be a fitting way to bring the book closure.

Intake: We shall call him Adam, and I will say that this guy enchanted me, not for the reason he was referred (too many people face the divorce crisis unfortunately), but due to three other reasons. First, he asked me to turn off both our cellular phones, stood up, grabbed my cell phone and his, and put them in my bag, which he put far aside. I was surprised, as I always put my phone on silent during the sessions. The guy, 43, explained to me that he did not want "external sources" to trace or listen to us. This surely sounded like a schizophrenic paranoid approach, yet the guy did not leave me with the impression that he was sick. Being a Masters graduate in mathematics and physics, with a wife and kids, driving an electric car ("not to pollute the air"), he offered me, by the end of the session, the payment in Bitcoins (the second reason I was surprised). That reassured my impression that, finally, after 40 years of psychotherapeutic practice, I had met the next millennium's client. I asked him politely to respect my 65 years of age, and allow me to be paid for my work with actual money, which he did, not before explaining to me, in detail how, in the very near future, I will convert paper bills to Bitcoins.

Now here is his story: Born to parents who lived a very modest life, as the father was a blacksmith and the mother a housewife, he was found gifted, and graduated from the best university in his homeland, continuing to a career working with artificial intelligence. Travelling through Europe, he met a young woman. Although sex was not a highlight, he said, she fitted all other criteria and they married and brought up their children, living in the countryside. Meanwhile, he continued a successful career in computer science. Recently, after 16 years of marriage, the wife fell in love with an artist (few years younger) and their marriage was about to collapse. He added that he suffered from lower back pains. I asked him how he felt about his wife's love affair, and he said, "First I was sad, and then I could feel the joy of potential freedom." He did mention that he was surprised that, last week, he saw a movie in which there was an erotic scene, and he was astonished that he was not sexually aroused. I told him it was quite reasonable that, in the midst of a marriage crisis, while the wife was away with her lover, he did not feel erotically aroused, and he looked at me quite stunned and muttered: "I don't see the connection" (my third surprise). He left, and we agreed on a sequence of sessions to start short-term therapy.

The next morning, I got a Whatsapp message: "Thanks a lot for the help. What about Arts, maybe through drawing or any other way I could release, or arrive at layers that right now are hidden from me, at least verbally?" Wow, I said to myself, he must have googled me...

What can we possibly make of this Intake?

Based on the holistic principle of Gestalt therapy, we can infer that Adam is a "mind freak," mainly approaching his life rationally. His emotional field of experience is hardly involved in his decision-making processes. He reported his back pain, and lately he's suffered severe pains. The body shouts for help, yet he does not attribute the physical suffering to his crisis, nor does he attribute his lack of libido to the humiliating events he has gone through during the last months. From a Jungian point of view, his wife is (in my impression) "animus possessed." He claimed that what intrigued him in her was "her integrity and bright mind." As long as they both were investing in self-actualizations (career, real estate, children) they fit together, but once these achievements had been fulfilled, a crack in the couple's relationship emerged. Eventually, into the system entered the lover, very likely an "Anima developed" man as he is an artist. The lover has a '"role" in their lives, and apparently appeared in the couple's life to develop the wife's femininity.

Unfortunately, Adam will discover his feminine side through inevitable suffering. He will need to go through a process of change, now that his wife intended to leave him. The paranoid approach to life is a sign that the high level of intelligence and intellect are not sufficient, when the emotional intelligence is short of processing the challenges Adam is confronted with. From Object Relations theory, we can infer that Adam suffers from a lack of empathic skills to relate to himself adequately, and likewise he does not relate to his wife. He is narcissistically wounded, but is unable to help himself. From a Jungian psychology point of view, we may claim that Adam is intuitively connected to his "wounded healer" archetype, *which pushed him to meet me in search of help.*

Session #2: Adam arrives to my studio and after a brief report he says it is quite strange for him to meet again as he thought I could have given him advice in the previous meeting which could have helped him solve "his marriage problem." I said I did give him advice, since I offered him to consider therapy and go on meeting with me and here he was, so I asked him to approach the art buffet to pick up some magazines and cut out few pictures which could describe his mood these days. Whistling to himself, he sets up for the assignment. He grabbed few magazines and glue and started scanning quite fast the pictures, tearing the selected pages fast and creating a pile near him. I recognized the melody he whistled and put on that melody through YouTube on my phone. Surprisingly, he said nothing about my use of the phone. "What now?" he asked, and I said: "Cut out the selected pictures and arrange them as a collage on the white paper I gave you." He took a "Japanese knife," cut each picture in square form and created a geometrical structure. "What do we have here?" I asked, and he said: "A man standing on a roof on top of a building, a garden full of organic vegetables, landscape at twilight and a person in surgery." Before I'd said a word, he added: "My father has cancer." I told him to choose one picture that calls for his attention most, and he chose the man on top of the roof. I said: "May I challenge you with a tough assignment which I believe can help you, will you agree to comply?" and he said: "Why then did I come here?" I asked him to pick up a chair and stand on top of it. He did. I asked him to repeat after me: "I am the person on top of the roof on top of the tall building." He looked at me as if I were nuts, smiled and repeated the sentence. I asked him to repeat that sentence three times. He did. "What do you feel," I asked. He said "nothing." I urged him to stand as close as possible to the edge of the chair. He did and started trembling. "What are you aware of?" I asked. He said, in a low voice: "My back hurts and it's quite scary." "Close your eyes and try to feel how it feels when everything is crushing around you, your marriage, your family and your Dad might be dying." His breathing was long, he shrunk and jumped off the chair saying: "Fuck you!, I understand." "What did you understand, dear Adam," I asked, and he put his head between his hands and tried hard to avoid tears. We sat close to each other and discussed, at length, the insights the experience granted us with. Adam was impressed with how standing on the edge of the chair had overwhelmed him, and connected him to the insight that he is losing control over his life. We realized that logic falls short of helping him overcome the overblown emotions which invade. Towards the end of the session, we talked about our partnership, as he said we have created a team to deal with his current life. He said we were now connected through "the big thing."

Let's analyze this second session: First, I suggest we look at the beginning of the session, when Adam complains to me for not helping him the previous time, and I "detour" from the confrontation: "I said I did, since I suggested he consider therapy and go on meeting with me, and here he was, so I asked him to approach the art buffet, to pick up some magazines and cut out a few pictures which described his mood these days." This is the power of the Expressive Arts Therapy & Coaching. Instead of dealing with the transference- counter transference aspects of our relationship, I refer Adam to the art buffet. He needs to deal with his issues through, with and along the artistic process. This is the added value of the

Expressive Arts Therapies or Coaching, as it prevents transference projections and directs the person inwards. Next, let me point to the theoretical concepts that came up throughout the session. Adam went into a short Creation Axis. The Contact and Organization were short, effective and task-oriented. We observed that he hardly enjoys the process, but rather executes the instructions, not allowing himself to surrender to the experience. He sorts out the pictures from the magazines as quickly as possible, and shows that he is dependent on the therapist, by asking: "What's next?" The form of the cut-out pictures is square, precise, as if documents are being presented. There is no internal need for integration or composition, no need for relatedness, the motivation is not intrinsic, and it lacks compassion. He is mainly obedient to the therapist's instructions. He skips the Improvisation - Phase and the Main Theme presents a collection of pictures which reveal danger, a dark mood and vulnerability. Diagnostically, the collage presents "Bad Content" expressed through a "Basic limited Form." "Bad content," because the man (in the picture) is attempting suicide, standing on the roof of a building, the landscape at twilight displays melancholy, and a person in surgery obviously hints at possible anxiety connected to his father's cancer. When the content is "bad" and the form is "good," we can infer that the client is post-traumatic, and indeed, this is Adam's situation when starting therapy.

In the Elaboration Phase, after having chosen the suicidal scene, I decided to shift into movement body work and revive the selected picture displaying the man on the edge of a building's roof. From Gestalt theory, we can point out several concepts: Figure and Ground, Holism (body work), Polarities and Awareness. From Expressive Therapy: Aesthetic Distancing. From Object

Relations: Empathy and Self object. Adam arrived at the second session "flooded" with life events. The technique of Aesthetic Distancing allows him, through the collage, to sort out all the problems which preoccupied him at the beginning of the session ("Ground"), and focus deeply and experientially on one ("Figure") - which creates the Main Theme of the session.

Another figure and ground principle is used when I ask Adam to sort out, from the collage (background), one picture (figure), and he selects the man on top of the building. We see here that the client's psyche (Jung) knows how to choose for the client what he should concentrate on. Selecting the right picture, which serves Adam best in the session, proves that Adam is connected to the archetype of the inner "wounded healer" (internal unconscious therapeutic instinct), which guides him through the challenging assignment of dealing with a particular aspect of his existential dilemmas. The art mediates between Adam and me, and prevents transference obstacles where Adam may project onto me his frustration, meaning that he chooses for himself what to focus on. The Gestalt approach helps bring to his awareness the terrible stress he experiences when his life is falling apart. By choosing the picture with the man on top of the roof, he invited himself to experience (on a body level) how fragile and vulnerable he was during that time. I applied the principle of Polarities by inviting Adam to stand on the edge of the chair. The "edge" is a life experience for Adam. Usually, people who are detached from their emotional intelligence need, inevitably, to go through tough or dangerous experiences, so that they can start heeding to their life's nuances. His back pain problems are signs of alarm. Now on the edge of the chair, he finally experiences that his life is falling apart, a fact he *preferred to deny emotionally. I use the dramatic aspects of the session to help us create a cradle for his baby "Self" (Jung), meaning Adam is exposed to aspects of his life through the emotional stanza, and needs protection and containment from my side (Object Relations).*

Session #3: Adam reports that efforts are being made on "both sides" (his wife and himself) to find, as soon as possible, a practical solution for their separation. When asked how was it to meet with me again, he answered by pulling out three books he had purchased (books I had recommended to him, upon his request in the first meeting) and presented them proudly, as if declaring: I am a good student, am I not!. He told me that, in the period between our previous meeting and this one, he had gone to two more different healers, in the search of relief from his stress. The first one was a medium who'd told him a "bad eye" had been put on his marriage, and she claimed she had taken that curse off. The second meeting was with a spiritual priest. That meeting had left him with relative compassion towards his wife, who may have found her real love in life. But the most intriguing issue he had brought up was the idea of building a new house in the village where they live, and share life with his wife and lover, so that the children would not suffer.

I decided to share with him my analysis of his present situation. Considering that he was a very rational person, I thought that, if we could share my assumptions and diagnostic impressions of his life crises, I might get better collaboration from him. I told him that, in my opinion, his masculine traits (on which he has been leaning most his life) are falling short of helping in this period of his life, in the sense that he is analyzing every database possible, rushing into decisions, looking for rational solutions, however paradoxically, and at the same time, his feminine side is in panic: He is searching for help in domains he would have never arrived at under normal circumstances, the domain of irrational experiences, starting with me as Clinical Expressive Arts therapist, and continuing with a medium and a priest. I said that we should look carefully and patiently into the process he is experiencing. I encouraged him to accept his feelings and to look into them. I said that suffering is in the essence of change, therefore he should not try to shorten the crises by inventing artificial solutions, but rather observe and contain the events and the suffering which follows. I explained how I think his wife is "Animus possessed," and how her femininity is being cured by her "anima lover." Meanwhile, I said, he is obliged to go into a process where he will, inevitably and gradually, develop his anima, which now is evoked.

When exposed to these "weird" concepts – as he labeled them, I invited him to create a Jungian sand tray. Shelves loaded with pre-arranged miniatures, laid out in categories on the shelves, and a large sand tray table welcomed his regressive child-like enthusiasm. I was impressed with how easily and quickly he surrendered to this experience. He spoke directly to the objects, in a nurturing voice, as if he were a child.

Here is the chronology of his sand tray process: Adam immediately created, in the sand, two identical hills, which seem to represent a symbolic woman's bosom. Across those roundish hills, he dug a small pond. Claiming that two curved lines symbolize two roads from the pond to the hills, he unconsciously created a feminine body image in the sand.

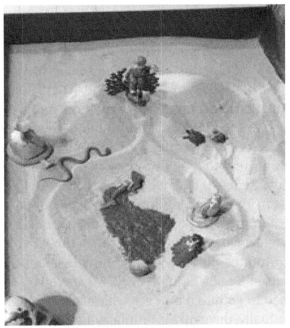

 Then he inserted a whole gallery of feminine figurines, starting with an Esmeralda dancing miniature located at the shore of the pond, nearby two other feminine figurines and a mermaid lying on the shore.

In between the sand hills' bosom, he located a very creative combination of a colorful peacock and a child riding on it. Along the shore's pond, he added a snake and two turtles. On the right hand side of Esmeralda, he placed a tiny owl.

Close to him, on the two corners of the tray, he located, on the left, a pig, and on the right, a matrioshka (Russian nesting dolls, representing his family). I told him that I was impressed by his innocent and naïve approach to the assignment. I was touched to see how the evoked anima was leading him to tell us an unconscious story, and how beautifully he personified the little miniatures, talking to them as if they were alive. He explained that he meant nothing while arranging the miniatures and the matrioshka contains one doll inside another and inside another, and this is "how my small family is to me."

Here is my Jungian analysis of the sand tray, and the importance of this activity in developing Adam's feminine side, which is so essential for coping with this life crises, as he is required to contain, process his feelings, and lean on undeveloped intuition. The fact that Adam paid attention and invested energy in the sand infrastructure is a sign that he does possess the ability to touch life from its roots and deal with basic instincts. He, spontaneously and unconsciously, sculptured in the sand a "Goddess Matriarchal Mother," which is a symbolic basis curved and piled from the soft sand. The blue pond, dug into the sand, created a feminine uterus, right at the correct location in the woman's symbolic body. The positive regression of a child's attitude caused him to talk directly to the miniatures he picked up from the shelves. It connected to the Buberian Gestalt principle of the I-Thou, where the client identifies, from zero distance, with the artistic artifact, in this case the miniatures. This proved an ability to empathize with the other, and nurture the other's needs.

Esmeralda was his first choice. She symbolizes manic defense, the need to be active, lively, joyful and charming, in order to cover up the suffering and fear he is experiencing. The other two casual feminine miniatures, he said, represented potential women to meet, as his wife had given up on him. The mermaid may represent his undeveloped Anima, lying on the "uterus" shore.

Of big importance is the child riding a peacock, a surrealistic combination. The child may represent Adam's under-developed masculinity, or newly-born Self, an emotional Self which corresponds to the Puer Eternus Archetype. This archetypal image represents the first stage of masculine development. According to Barbara Greenfield, in her article: "The Archetypal Masculine: It's Manifestation in Myth, and Its Significance for Women" (in The Father: Contemporary Jungian Perspectives, Ed. Samuels Andrew, 1985, Free Association Books, London), there are six stages of development for men's masculinity: The Child = Peur Eternus, Don Juan, Trickster, Hero, Father and the Xenex - the wise old man. The family's crisis pushed Adam into a regression towards a new immature childish Self. The peacock signifies both Masculinity and also the potential of the "Self," as it can impress, expand and enchant, as the peacock tail opens up. The condensation of the two into a combined sculpture grants stronger proof of the inevitable regression, with the promise of a developmental experience.

If we summarize the sand tray as a predictive creative day dream, we can assume that Adam is, indeed, at the beginning of a transformative phase.

We discussed, at length, the practical derivate of developing an Anima, and what the growing of the Self meant. Meanwhile, Adam agreed to hold off on building a new house on his farm, and agreed to go on with the therapy process, without making hasty decisions.

Session # 4: Held as a conversation, this session was a kind of a late Intake, where I learned about Adam and his wife's nuclear families.

Session # 5: Adam creates his own hand, using gypsum bandages.

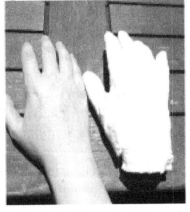

The process is tedious, as it is quite challenging to make one's own hand with this technique. When absolutely necessary, I helped Adam. I promoted the idea of working with gypsum as a response to Adam's comment, right in the beginning of the session, that he felt like he had gone through a car accident. "Everything in my life," he'd claimed, is "totally lost." I thought that a curative experience could connect Adam with self-compassion and self-remorse, trying to support him in enduring the tedious life challenges he was experiencing.

When Adam finished creating the gypsum glove, I asked him to create a dialogue between the gypsum hand and his own hand, which was located near the gypsum one.

Adam's hand: "It was quite hard to create you."
Gypsum hand: "Yet I came out quite perfect."
Adam's hand: "I had to work carefully and go on, layer by layer."
Gypsum hand: "Yes, and you had to stick together so many pieces to assemble me."
Adam's hand: "What do you need now?"
Gypsum hand: "Paint me, make me happy, fill me with something, let me hold something."
Adam's hand: "I like you the way you are, white and clean."
Gypsum hand: "You want me to be simple?"
Adam's hand: "I want you to be the way I created you."
I suggested that Adam look into this dialogue, and we analyzed it together, to see how the conversation corresponds to his life. In the beginning, I told Adam, the dialogue referred to the creation of the gypsum glove. You said it was hard, and you had to put layer upon layer. What does it mean to you, referring it to your current life experiences? Adam said: "It seems, in life, I am destroying, and here I construct." I said: "Yes, and constructing is harder than destructing."

Adam stopped, turned sad and bent inwards. I joined his silence. He started to cry, caressing the gypsum hand slowly. After a while, he stared at me and, with a low voice, said: "How can I cure the wound? How can I save my family?" I referred to the second part of the dialogue, and pointed out that the gypsum hand wanted to become colorful and functional. But Adam insisted on not complying with the hand's wish, but rather keeping it white. I asked Adam what this meant to him. He said: "It's all about showing off. All my life, I was busy, seeking to succeed and show off my achievements. Now the family crisis pushes me into deep shit. A hole, a deep hole, with nothing to be proud of."

I said that I was impressed at how much patience he displayed while creating the gypsum glove, and I connected those efforts to the efforts required to try put together his family. I offered an option to meet with his wife, him and me together, now that she was back home with the kids. He looked stunned and said:" Do you think there is a chance?" I said that we have not tried yet, and asked him whether he assumed his wife would comply with such an invitation. He said he should really check. We departed with a certain hope that we might onset a dialogue within the couple.

Let us analyze this fifth session. The art project checks Adam's ability to invest in the object. The therapeutic intervention lies in the principle of creating Object Relations with an object which very likely will frustrate, challenge and annoy Adam. Diagnostically, the final artistic outcome shows "good form" with "good content." Adam elaborates on his relationship. The creation of the gypsum hand brings to the therapeutic space an opportunity to experience an artistic Self -Object. He created an extension of his Self and, through the Buberian I-Thou Dialogue (Gestalt), he was able to differentiate and discover a vulnerable part in his personality which he wished to change. Through the personification of the gypsum hand, Adam discovered that it wishes to show off colorfully, and be granted self-efficiency ("paint me, make me happy, fill me with something, let me hold something"). However, Adam wanted it to be simple and authentic. This shows a certain change in Adam's Object Relations. He stands for his True Self and tries to avoid a "False Self presented glove." He said: "I like you the way you are, white and clean." In Jungian terms, Adam lived "an ego-inflated" life. Now, facing a crisis, a humbleness is required, which is a preliminary condition for an authentic approach to negotiation. The shift from a dual dialogue between two hands to a potential dialogue with the challenging wife is obvious, and creates a certain hope. Once a shift from the "Doing" position into the "Being" position is acquired, I thought it seemed worthwhile to try to open the therapeutic space to the couple in crisis.

At this point, dear reader, we shall depart. We do hope that, by the end of this intellectual and emotional quest, you have acquired an innovative point of view towards Clinical Expressive Arts Therapies and Coaching. Nearby, on your private library's shelf, you may add my upcoming book *Psychodynamic Snapshots of Clinical Expressive Arts Therapy: Theory and Practice*, soon to be published by Cambridge Scholars Press, a book which will add an even deeper level of comprehension to the theoretical issues we have exposed in this present book.

Index

A
Aesthetic Distancing 233,234
Amodal Perception 110,113, 115, 116, 117, 118
anal 218, 219, 220, 221, 222, 223
artifact 64, 90, 91, 96, 101, 117, 123, 124, 125, 127, 136, 137, 138, 140, 154, 156, 163, 173, 183, 185, 187, 193, 213, 215, 216, 217, 219, 220, 222, 239
awareness 17, 18, 24, 42, 47, 53, 57, 59, 97, 109, 121, 136, 137, 172, 186, 234

B
Bion 104, 106, 107, 143
Biran 104, 143
Bollas 13, 120, 138, 143
Buber 101

C
center 46, 55, 85, 185, 186, 187, 188, 191
change 45, 47, 48, 49, 85, 88, 98, 100, 102, 107, 120, 121, 134, 171, 205, 209, 230, 236, 243, 244
Chronology 213
color 28, 37, 57, 82, 109, 132, 163, 165, 166, 167, 168, 169, 171, 212
component 130, 192, 202, 211, 212, 213, 223
concrete 9, 53, 80, 81, 84, 86
confrontation 232
conscious 8, 9, 11, 17, 32, 34, 53, 186, 204
Contact 133, 157, 233

Creation Axis 23, 24, 37, 60, 64, 67, 68, 75, 81, 82, 91, 101, 103, 107, 117, 118, 127, 132, 138, 139, 141, 152, 153, 154, 157, 162, 168, 174, 175, 179, 182, 188, 200, 201, 213, 233

D
Depressive Position 82, 83, 84, 85, 86, 87, 88, 98, 102
depth 12, 15, 96, 116, 162, 194, 211, 222
Destruction of the Object 98, 99, 101
diagnostic conclusion 148, 149
diagnostic thought 66, 148, 149, 151, 199, 211, 213
differential diagnosis 96, 170
dimension 154, 155, 157, 158, 161, 168, 170, 188, 213, 214, 233
direction 95, 116, 157, 163, 195, 196, 205, 206, 208
distancing 81, 84
dream 10, 13, 16, 54, 55, 56, 59, 61, 63, 34, 66, 85, 106, 241

E
Elaboration 152, 174, 182, 233
emotion 25, 171
empathy 120, 121, 131, 133
episode 65

F
False Self 62, 92, 94, 95, 96, 99, 118, 144, 244,
Fascination 122
femininity 16, 28, 29, 127, 167,

186, 216, 230, 236
focus 34, 54, 66, 188, 189, 199, 211, 233, 234
focusing 183, 185, 187, 188,
Form 163, 164, 165, 168, 170, 174, 175, 176, 177, 178, 180, 181, 183, 184, 185, 208, 216, 233

G

Gegorian 167
generalization 161
Genital 218
Giacometti 159, 219
Goren-Bar 1, 167

H

Here & Now 43, 57, 63, 66
hint 22, 38, 43, 66, 155, 188, 189, 194, 197, 200, 202, 209
Holism 233

I

icon 124
Improvisation 36, 60, 81, 85, 157, 184, 185, 200, 201, 233
integration 67, 160, 161, 191, 192, 193, 233
intentional communication 111, 1112
internalized image 78
interpretation 54, 208
interval 197

K

Klein 76, 77, 80, 83, 84, 89, 92, 106, 126, 128, 143, 144
Kohut 50, 109, 119, 120, 121, 122, 125, 126, 130, 131, 138, 141, 142, 143, 144, 184

Kreitler 163, 165, 224

L

Latent Potential 150
Levine 70, 72
line 23, 112, 140, 148, 180, 190, 195, 197, 198, 199, 200, 203, 205, 206, 207, 208, 212
location 185, 186, 184, 239

M

Main Theme 23, 47, 60, 102, 107, 137, 138, 139, 141, 157, 174, 175, 176, 178, 179, 184, 185, 186, 191, 200, 201, 204, 221, 233, 234
material 16, 26, 33, 60, 150, 157, 159, 160, 161, 165, 184, 188, 193, 194, 214, 215, 219, 222
meaning 7, 8, 9, 11, 12, 19, 23, 24, 25, 30, 31, 35, 38, 42, 43, 48, 50, 58, 63, 67, 69, 70, 75, 78, 79, 85, 86, 88, 89, 97, 99, 105, 110, 115, 116, 118, 120, 121, 122, 124, 132, 134, 135, 140, 149, 150, 155, 156, 163, 165, 166, 167, 173, 179, 180, 185, 195, 196, 202, 205, 207, 210, 212, 223, 234, 235
Miller 92, 144
mirroring 78, 113, 190
mood 57, 84, 223, 231, 232, 233
motion 195, 196, 197

N

Netzer 46, 72
Neumann 8, 12, 50, 72, 167, 224
norm 119, 150, 166, 179

O

Object Relations 3, 13, 75, 76, 77, 78, 80, 82, 84, 86, 88, 90, 91, 92, 94, 96, 98, 100, 102, 104, 106, 109, 111, 113, 115, 117, 119, 121, 123, 125, 127, 129, 133, 135, 137, 139, 141, 143, 144, 178, 201, 230, 233, 235, 243, 244
Ogden 103, 111, 120, 144
Optimal Frustration 122
Organization 152, 153, 157, 184, 233

P

Parental Image 76, 77, 78, 79, 82, 83, 84, 88, 89, 90, 97, 93, 94, 100, 104, 105, 111, 122, 125, 127, 136, 138
Pointillism 205
Polarities 15, 215, 233, 234
pole 39, 56, 57, 58, 59, 60, 61, 63, 87, 134, 137, 180
potential space 197
Preservation 64, 101, 103, 107, 168
Primitive Edge of Experience 103, 111, 144
process 13, 14, 15, 16, 18, 19, 20, 33, 34, 35, 39, 42, 43, 46, 48, 49, 54, 67, 82, 84, 85, 90, 91, 100, 102, 106, 120, 122, 126, 129, 132, 133, 136, 138, 148, 160, 161, 167, 171, 176, 178, 180, 184, 192, 200, 206, 213, 214, 223, 228, 230, 232, 233, 236, 23, 241
prototype 200, 201, 202, 203, 204, 205, 206, 207, 208, 210, 212, 213, 222

R

repetition 190, 206, 209, 212, 220
Reverie 106

S

sand tray 28, 40, 55, 56, 68, 69, 191, 196, 216, 236, 239, 241
Secret 48, 67, 71, 88, 115, 151, 156, 210, 211, 222, 223, 224
sharing 152
Simplicity 104, 143
stages 75, 89, 99, 110, 131, 132, 157, 213, 240
Sublimation 177
surrogate 127, 138, 142

T

three times 231
True Self 13, 62, 92, 94, 95, 96, 97, 98, 99, 123, 201, 244
trust 43, 58, 82, 116

U

Unity of the Senses 109

V

Vitality Affect 114, 115

W

Winnicott 41, 85, 92. 94, 98, 99, 101, 103, 119, 120, 122, 137, 143, 144

Made in the USA
Monee, IL
18 December 2023

48282900R00138